EFFECTS OF CATASTROPHIC EVENTS ON TRANSPORTATION SYSTEM MANAGEMENT AND OPERATIONS

New York City—September 11, 2001

April 21, 2002

U.S. Department of Transportation
ITS Joint Program Office

Technical Report Documentation Page

1. Report No.	2. Government Accession No.	3. Recipient's Catalog No.

4. Title and Subtitle	5. Report Date
Effects of Catastrophic Events on Transportation System Management and Operations, New York City – September 11	April 2002
	6. Performing Organization Code

7. Author(s)	8. Performing Organization Report No.
Allan J. DeBlasio, Terrance J. Regan, Margaret E. Zirker, F. Brian Day, Michelle Crowder, Kathleen Bagdonas, Robert Brodesky, Dan Morin	

9. Performing Organization Name and Address	10. Work Unit No. (TRAIS)
U.S. Department of Transportation Research and Special Programs Administration Volpe National Transportation Systems Center 55 Broadway Cambridge, MA 02142-1093	
	11. Contract or Grant No.

12. Sponsoring Agency Name and Address	13. Type of Report and Period Covered
U.S. Department of Transportation Federal Highway Administration ITS Joint Program Office 400 Seventh Street, SW Washington, DC 20590	Catastrophic Events Case Study
	14. Sponsoring Agency Code

15. Supplementary Notes

Contracting Officer's Technical Representative (COTR) – Joseph Peters

16. Abstract

This report documents the actions taken by transportation agencies in response to the earthquake in Northridge, California on January 17, 1994, and is part of a larger effort to examine the impacts of catastrophic events on transportation system facilities and services. The findings documented in this report are a result of a detailed literature search on Northridge lessons learned. As part of a larger effort, four case studies will be produced:

- New York City, September 11, 2001
- Washington, D.C., September 11, 2001
- Baltimore, Maryland, rail tunnel fire, July 18, 2001
- Northridge, California, earthquake, January 17, 1994.

17. Key Word	18. Distribution Statement
Emergency Response, Emergency Preparedness, Security, Transportation System Recovery, Disaster, Catastrophic Event, Terrorist Attack	No restrictions

19. Security Classif. (of this report)	20. Security Classif. (of this page)	21. No. of Pages	22. Price
Unclassified	Unclassified		

Form DOT F 1700.7 (8 72)   Reproduction of completed page authorized

Foreword

This report was prepared by the U.S. Department of Transportation's (U.S. DOT) John A. Volpe National Transportation Systems Center (Volpe Center) for the U.S. DOT's Intelligent Transportation Systems (ITS) Joint Program Office. The Volpe Center study team consisted of Allan J. DeBlasio, the project manager; Robert Brodesky from EG&G Technical Services; Margaret E. Zirker and Michelle Crowder from Cambridge Systematics Inc.; and Terrance J. Regan, F. Brian Day, Kathleen Bagdonas, and Dan Morin from Planners Collaborative. Vince Pearce is the U.S. DOT task manager of the review.

This report documents the actions taken by transportation agencies in response to the terrorist attack in New York City on September 11, and is part of a larger effort to examine the impacts of catastrophic events on transportation system facilities and services. The findings documented in this report are a result of the creation of a detailed chronology of New York events, a literature search, and interviews of key personnel involved in transportation operations decision-making on September 11. As part of a larger effort, four case studies will be produced:

- New York City, September 11, 2001
- Washington, D.C., September 11, 2001
- Baltimore, Maryland, rail tunnel fire, July 18, 2001
- Northridge, California, earthquake, January 17, 1994.

Each of these events resulted in substantial, immediate, and adverse impacts on transportation, and each has had varying degrees of influence on the longer-term operation of transportation facilities and services in their respective region. Each event revealed important information about the response of the transportation system to major stress and the ability of operating agencies and their public safety and emergency management partners to respond effectively to a crisis. This report emphasizes the transportation aspects of this catastrophic event and lessons learned that could be incorporated into future emergency response planning.

Contents

Table of Contents

1.0 Introduction 1

    2.0 Transportation System Response 3

    2.1 Pre-Event 3

    2.2 Day of Event: September 11, 2001 7

    2.3 Post-Event: After September 11, 2001 21

3.0 Findings 31

    3.1 Advance Preparations and Planning 34

    3.2 Institutional Coordination 38

    3.3 Guiding Priority: Safety 41

    3.4 Communications 42

    3.5 The Role of Advanced Technologies 45

    3.6 System Redundancy and Resiliency 49

4.0 Conclusion 51

List of Acronyms 53

List of Tables

Table 1. Regional Statistics 3

Table 2. Weekday Transit Ridership 4

Table 3. Journey to Work by Mode for Manhattan 6

Table 4. Key Decisions by Agency 18

List of Figures

Figure 1. VMS Sign on Sept. 11 1

Figure 2. World Trade Center Complex, Mid-September 2

Figure 3. Transportation Conditions Before Sept. 11 5

Figure 4. Pedestrians Crossing the Brooklyn Bridge from Manhattan ... 7

Figure 5. Looking South Down West Street on September 11 11

Figure 6. Transportation Conditions on September 11 12

List of Figures (continued)

Figure 7. Ambulances on a Manhattan Street on September 11 14

Figure 8. Ferry Passengers on September 11 16

FIgure 9. Day-After Newspaper Map 20

Figure 10. New York City Transit Map of September 24 21

Figure 11. Transportation Conditions, late Fall 2001 26

Figure 12. Effect of SOV Ban on Traffic 28

Figure 13. Ferry Service, late Fall 2001 30

Figure 14. Subway Station on Morning of Sept.ember 11 37

Figure 15. Increase in Web Usage Sept. 11 44

Figure 16 Subway Service Notice September 17 45

Figure 17. VMS on Evening of September 11 46

Figure 18. IRVN Screen Shot 47

1.0 Introduction

Although New York City transportation agencies never planned for an attack of the magnitude of September 11, they swung into action without hesitation, implementing individual and regional emergency response plans already in place. Within 6 minutes of the first hijacked airliner crash into the north tower of the World Trade Center in New York City, both New York City Transit subways and Port Authority Trans-Hudson (PATH) trains began emergency procedures. Within 9 minutes of a second hijacked airliner crash into the south tower of the World Trade Center, the Port Authority of New York and New Jersey closed all bridges and tunnels and the George Washington Bridge variable message sign (VMS) flashed, "Bridge Closed." (See September 11, 2001 Chronology—The First Hour.)

For the next several hours, over 1 million people who live and work in lower Manhattan fled. New York City Mayor Rudy Giuliani told New Yorkers, "If you are south of Canal Street, get out. Walk slowly and carefully. If you can't figure what else to do, just walk north." Shaken from the terror, people headed north to find transportation options that were still operating or toward the water where they could cross bridges on foot or board the make-shift flotilla of water ferries that was quickly mobilized to transport people off the island. As the region's three major airports were closed, people began walking with their luggage, hitchhiking, or commandeering airport luggage carts to begin a search for buses, rental cars, and hotels.

However, in the chaos and devastation of the seemingly unmanageable disaster, the New York transportation system remained a support system for those fleeing the tragedy and for those charged with on-site emergency response. Throughout the chaos of the day, the New York transportation system adapted to serve travelers and keep them safe on September 11.

Sensitivity

These findings of the impacts of the September 11 attacks are being compiled only months after the most damaging terrorist attack in American history. For this reason, there are a number of sensitivities surrounding the case study work. The World Trade Center area is still considered a crime scene, and the Federal Bureau of Investigation (FBI) is coordinating activities and responses. Because of the nature of the terrorist attack, officials at the time could not be sure that additional terrorist activities would not occur in the region. Transportation officials were (and still are) concerned about the targeting of their facilities. Therefore, some of the information remains classified and officials are reticent to discuss details of certain responses and actions that took place that day.

Because of the nature of the incident, some of the interviewees were reluctant to share detailed information about possible changes in emergency response

Figure 1. VMS Sign on Sept. 11
Source: Port Authority

plans for fear of giving would-be terrorists a "blueprint" for how to better plan the next attack. The World Trade Center was the headquarters for a number of the transportation agencies and a communications hub. Many of the key agency officials were actually at the site at the time of the attack. A number of the high-ranking decision makers for the transportation agencies were either killed or temporarily lost during the first few hours after the attack. Most everyone interviewed told a personal story of close friends lost or of their own narrow escape from injury or death. Many of the agency personnel have been working long hours to operate the system under tremendous constraints and have not had time to "debrief and reflect on lessons learned."

Figure 2. World Trade Center Complex, Mid-September
Source: FEMA

2.0 Transportation System Response

2.1 Pre-Event

New York City, Manhattan, and Lower Manhattan

New York City is the most populous city in the nation. The borough of Manhattan, 13-miles long and 2.3-miles wide at its widest point, holds only 7% of the land area of New York City, but 20% of the total population. Manhattan is the most densely populated urban area in the country. It is also one of the most visited tourist destinations in the world. Lower Manhattan, the area below 14th Street, was home to the World Trade Center Complex. Table 1 gives an overview of statistics for New York City, Manhattan and Lower Manhattan.

Table 1. Regional Statistics

	NYC	Manhattan	Lower Manhattan
Population	8,800,000	1,537,000	292,000
Workers	3,700,000	2,400,000	566,000
Area (sq. mi.)	309	28	3
Density of residents per sq. mi.	28,479	54,893	97,333
Density of employees per sq. mi.	11,974	85,714	188,667
% households owning a vehicle	44%	22%	—

Transportation in New York City and Manhattan

The New York metropolitan area, which includes the 2,440 square-mile region of New York City, Long Island, and the lower Hudson Valley, has one of the most extensive transportation networks in the world with nearly 23,000 centerline miles of roads, streets, and highways, approximately 500 route-miles of commuter rail, 225 route-miles of rail rapid transit, three major airports, and the largest maritime facilities for passengers and goods on the East Coast.

The transportation system in New York City is one of the most complex in the country with innumerable state, local, and regional authorities as well as private companies operating various components of the transportation network. The three largest public transportation agencies that serve New York City are:

- ◆ The Port Authority of New York and New Jersey, which operates the 3 major airports, 2 tunnels, 4 bridges, the PATH interstate passenger rail transit system, 2 interstate bus terminals, and 7 marine cargo terminals in the New York/New Jersey Port District.

- ◆ The NYC Department of Transportation (DOT), which manages the city streets, highways, parking facilities, 4 major bridges, 6 tunnels, 1 ferry service, and oversees 5 private ferry and 7 private bus companies serving New York City.

- The Metropolitan Transportation Authority (MTA) runs the NYC Transit subway and bus system (the largest subway and bus systems in the country), 2 commuter rail systems, a Long Island bus service, 7 bridges, and 2 tunnels.

According to the Texas Transportation Institute's indices of roadway congestion, the region ranked 13th in percent of daily travel undertaken in congested conditions, 21st in roadway congestion, and 24th in annual congestion cost per capita. These rankings reflect a 35% share of daily travel undertaken in congested conditions and an annual congestion cost of $595 per capita.

Within New York City itself, there are about 2 million registered vehicles, 91% of which are passenger vehicles, 4% commercial vehicles, 2.5% taxis, and the remaining 2.5 % rental cars, buses, and motorcycles/mopeds. Figure 3 on the following page gives a brief overview of transportation conditions before September 11, 2001.

The New York metropolitan area has the most widely used public transportation network in the nation. The region's reliance on transit stems from historical trends and land use patterns, principally in New York City where the density makes automobile travel difficult. The largest portion of the city's transit system is operated by MTA NYC Transit. From outside the city, MTA's commuter rail and bus operations serve suburban New York including Long Island, the Hudson River Valley, and parts of Connecticut; PATH rapid transit brings passengers to NYC from New Jersey; ferries connect other New York City boroughs with Manhattan, as well as carrying passengers from New Jersey. Table 2 shows the typical weekday transit ridership statistics for the New York City area.

Table 2. Weekday Transit Ridership

Transit type	Passengers/weekday
NYC Transit subway	4,226,600
NYC Transit buses	2,169,800
Private buses	288,900
MTA Long Island Bus	99,100
MTA Long Island Railroad	296,800
MTA Metro North Railroad	231,600
Port Authority PATH	258,000
Public and private ferries	91,600
TOTAL	7,662,400

Source: NYMTC and Port Authority

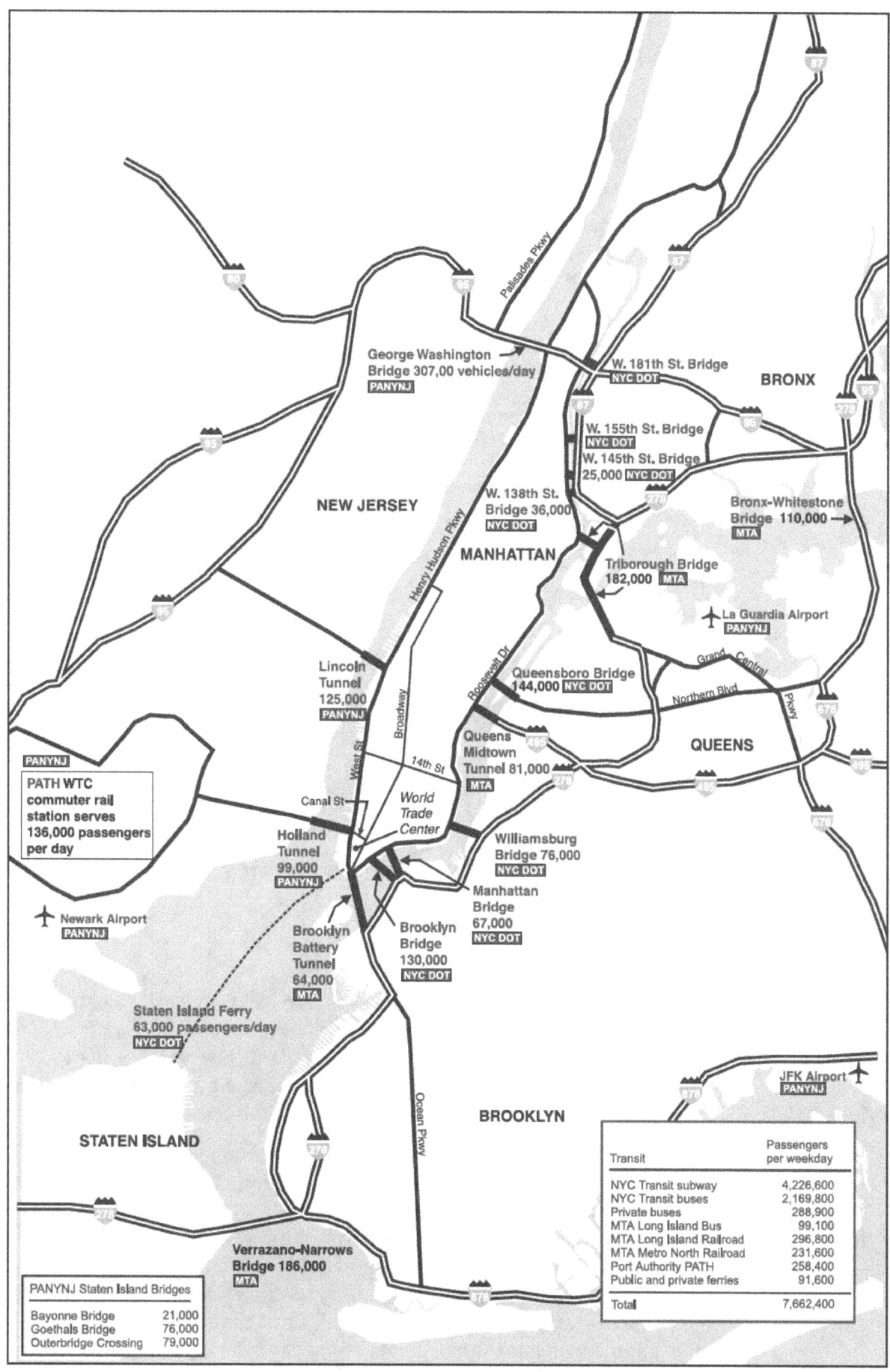

Figure 3. Transportation Conditions Before September 11

Transportation in Manhattan

Most people who work in Manhattan take transit or walk. Only 16% of all workers rely on the automobile to commute to Manhattan. During the daytime, more than two-thirds of all trips in the 8.4 square miles that comprise central Manhattan are made on foot. Even so, 14,000 motor vehicle trips are made per square mile per day, far exceeding trip density of all other counties in the New York metropolitan area.

Table 3. Journey to Work by Mode for Manhattan

	Within Manhattan	From NYC	From NYC Suburbs	From NJ	From CT
SOV	4%	8%	21%	19%	12%
HOV (2+)	2%	4%	8%	10%	4%
Subway	38%	55%	5%	12%	2%
Bus	15%	12%	5%	35%	2%
Rail	<1%	2%	60%	22%	77%
Ferry	0%	1%	<1%	1%	0%
Taxicab	5%	2%	<1%	<1%	1%
Walk, Bicycle	27%	12%	<1%	<1%	2%
Other*	8%	4%	<1%	<1%	<1%
Total	100%	100%	100%	100%	100%

NYMTC Journey to Work Analysis, from 1990 census data

*Other includes all other modes of travel including work-at-home.

World Trade Center Complex

The World Trade Center Complex's seven buildings with its 293 floors of office space housed some 1,200 companies and organizations. Each floor of the Twin Towers contained over 1 acre of office space. The complex included 239 elevators and 71 escalators. The World Trade Center housed approximately 50,000 office workers and averaged 90,000 visitors each day.

The below-ground Mall was the largest enclosed shopping mall in Lower Manhattan as well as the main interior pedestrian circulation level for the World Trade Center complex. Approximately 150,000 people a day used the three subway stations located below the towers in the Mall. The below-ground parking garage included space for 2,000 vehicles, but only 1,000 were used on a daily basis. The number of parking spaces was reduced for safety and security reasons after terrorists drove a truck packed with 1,100 pounds of explosives into the basement parking garage in 1993, setting off a blast that killed 6 and injured 1,000 people.

Because of the terrorist bombing of the World Trade Center in 1993 and subsequent emergencies, such as the 1999 Queens electrical blackout and the 1995 Toyko Subway gas attack, the New York City region had dramatically increased its planning for major emergencies before September 11, 2001. The New York City Office of Emergency Management (OEM), under the direction of the New York City Mayor's office, significantly upgraded its resources and preparedness, including the completion of a new emergency command center in 1999 at 7 World Trade Center. OEM formed a task force to implement upgrades to the existing emergency response plans for the New York City region. The region used the incident command system (ICS). In addition to following the ICS, individual agencies upgraded their own internal emergency procedures.

The World Trade Center itself was upgraded after the 1993 bombing with over $90 million worth of safety improvements, including a duplicate source of power for safety equipment, such as fire alarms, emergency lighting and intercoms. Most importantly, building management took evacuation preparedness seriously, conducting evacuation drills every six months. Each floor had "fire wardens," sometimes high-ranking executives of a tenant, who were responsible for organizing and managing an evacuation of their floors. In part because of this preparedness, 99 percent of the occupants of each tower on the floors below the crashes survived.

Figure 4. Pedestrians Crossing the Brooklyn Bridge from Manhattan September 11, 2001 Chronology—The First Hour

2.2 Day of Event: September 11, 2001

The first airplane attack occurred during the morning rush hour when the city's roads, bridges, and transit system were operating at peak capacity. Lower Manhattan is a major work destination and is served by multiple subway and rail lines below ground and local and express buses above ground. There are five major river crossings below 14th Street carrying a total of 335,000 autos, buses, and other vehicles into the area daily. Transportation officials were immediately faced with the need to make critical decisions on how to respond in order to protect the safety of the traveling public. The decisions were made more difficult because of the circumstances that were unfolding at a rapid pace. Adding to the difficulty were the lack of accurate, immediate information about the implications and extent of the event, the inability to quickly communicate agency actions internally and externally, and the need to ensure the safety of their own transportation facilities in the event of possible follow-up attacks.

In the first few minutes there was a lack of accurate information and a sense of disbelief at the level of destruction. The media quickly broadcast images of the damage but did not have immediate information on the implications of the attack. As fires raged in the two buildings, vital utility and communications systems began to fail. Communications failures included the loss of numerous radio and communications towers located on top of the towers, the destruction of the Verizon and Port Authority communications hubs, and an overwhelming demand for those communications services that were still operational. As electrical power was lost to the area, traffic signals no longer worked, hindering traffic movement. The Brooklyn Battery Tunnel lost lighting and ventilation for the Manhattan portion of the tunnel, forcing motorists to abandon their cars in the tunnel as smoke and debris poured in. The loss of electricity made it more difficult to fight the fires resulting from the attack and to begin pumping operations to prevent flooding of underground transit and utility facilities.

September 11, 2001 Chronology—The First Hour

Time of Day	Elapsed Time	Event/Actions Taken
8:46 a.m.:		First plane crashes into the north tower of the World Trade Center (WTC).
8:47 a.m.:	[1 min.]	An MTA subway operator alerts MTA Subway Control Center of an explosion in the WTC and begins emergency procedures.
8:52 a.m.:	[6 min.]	PATH trains begin emergency procedures and proceed to evacuate WTC station and express Manhattan trains to New Jersey.
9:03 a.m.:	[17 min.]	Second plane crashes into south tower of WTC.
9:06 a.m.	[20 min.]	John F. Kennedy International Airport closes for departures, Laguardia Airport closes for all arrivals and departures at 9:07 and Newark Airport closes at 9:09.
9:10 a.m.:	[24 min.] eastbound.	Port Authority of NY and NJ closes all their bridges and tunnels
9:12 a.m.:	[26 min.]	George Washington Bridge VMS signs flash "Bridge Closed."
9:17 a.m.:	[31 min.]	FAA orders all NYC airports closed until further notice.
morning:		Amtrak suspends all nationwide train service; Greyhound cancels Northeast US operations.
morning:		NYC DOT reports that police ordered highways shut down.
9:40 a.m.:	[54 min.]	FAA halts all US flights.
9:43 a.m.:	[57 min.]	Third plane crashes into the Pentagon.
9:45 a.m.:	[59 min.]	The White House evacuates.

Within the first hour, each of the transportation agencies had begun internal emergency procedures and coordination with other agencies. Within minutes both NYC Transit and PATH had begun emergency operations and were evacuating transit stations in the World Trade Center area. In the case of NYC Transit, a subway train operator who had pulled his train into Cortlandt Station reported the impact of the first plane crash to Subway Operations 1 minute after the crash. Because of the implementation of emergency procedures protocol, this was the last train to use the station before it was destroyed in the collapse of the towers an hour and thirteen minutes later. The PATH system began similar procedures 6 minutes after the first plane hit ensuring that the World Trade Center station was evacuated and regular service was suspended before the PATH station was destroyed.

Under the coordination of the New York Police Department (NYPD), the Port Authority, MTA and the NYC DOT quickly implemented procedures to close all the bridge and tunnel crossings into Manhattan. New York and New Jersey police began the process of closing interstates with major access points into New York City. The FAA ordered the Port Authority to close all New York City airports.

TRANSCOM, a coalition of 16 transportation and public safety agencies in the New York metropolitan region, began the process of alerting other agencies of the status of facilities and providing updated transportation information to agencies all along the Northeast Corridor. As facilities were closed, agency personnel began performing vulnerability assessments of their own facilities.

While New York City transportation agencies had individual and regional emergency response plans in place, no one had planned for an attack of the magnitude of September 11. In addition to the loss of key emergency response and transportation personnel who worked in the command center, the transportation and communications networks in Lower Manhattan sustained substantial damage. The World Trade Center served as the major intermodal transportation hub for Lower Manhattan. The Cortlandt subway station and the PATH World Trade Center station were both severely damaged during the collapse of the Twin Towers. Communications hubs for Verizon, TRANSCOM, and the Port Authority as well as the MTA's fiber-optic network were all located either within or in close proximity to the World Trade Center. All of these were totally or partially destroyed, severing communications during the first few hours after the attack. This hindered the ability to communicate internally and externally during the first few critical hours.

Adding to the confusion in the first hour was the fact that several emergency controls centers, including the City's, FEMA's and the Port Authority's, were located in the World Trade Center complex. At 9:00 a.m., 14 minutes after the first plane crashed into the World Trade Center, city officials activated the city's OEM Emergency Operations Center at 7 World Trade Center. After hearing a voice on police radio and a second blast three minutes later, New York City OEM abandoned its 7 World Trade Center offices. The OEM found functioning phones at a Merrill Lynch office on 75 Barclay Street, about 1 block from 7 World Trade Center. OEM staff set to work immediately getting the White House on the phone and contacting other key members of the command team.

As the south tower of the World Trade Center collapsed at 10:05 a.m., the OEM fled its temporary Merrill Lynch location as the area became engulfed in dust, dirt and debris. They next set up command at a fire station in West Village, about a mile north of the Merrill Lynch location. After about an hour, lack of desks and insufficient space forced the team to leave the fire station in search of larger quarters.

Around 11:00 a.m., the New York City OEM moved its command center to the 6th Floor Library of the New York City Police Academy on 20th Street, about a mile north of the West Village location. Police Department technicians began running replacement phone lines into a few essential offices inside the NYC OEM makeshift command center at the Police Academy.

The Port Authority initially tried to set up a control center in the Marriott Hotel adjacent to the World Trade Center but they quickly had to abandon that site because of its proximity to the attack. After that they moved to an interim center in Jersey City from which they could communicate with Port Authority facilities and the City's OEM.

September 11, 2001 Chronology- Late Morning

Time of Day	Elapsed Time	Event/Actions Taken
9:59 a.m.:	[1 hr. 13 min.]	South tower of WTC collapses. Impact measures 2.1 on the Richter scale.
morning:		NY state activates its Emergency Operations Center in Albany. Governor activates the National Guard.
10:20 a.m.:	[1 hr. 34 min.]	NYC Transit suspends all subway service.
10:29 a.m.:	[1 hr. 43 min.]	North tower of WTC collapses. Impact measures 2.3 on the Richter scale. Port Authority headquarters destroyed in the collapse.
10:30 a.m.:	[1 hr. 44 min.]	NJ Transit stops rail service into Manhattan's Penn Station.
10:45 a.m.:	[1 hr. 59 min.]	PATH operations were suspended.
10:53 a.m.:	[2 hr. 7 min.]	NY primary elections are postponed.
11:02 a.m.:	[2 hr. 16 min.]	As tens of thousands abandon cars and subway to stream across Manhattan bridges on foot, Mayor Giuliani urges, "Stay calm, stay at home… If you are south of Canal Street, get out. Walk slowly and carefully. If you can't figure what else to do, just walk north."

By the second hour, a horrible event became even worse as the two towers began collapsing, spreading thousands of tons of debris and ash over Lower Manhattan. Visibility was diminished and breathing became difficult for those leaving the area as well as for those emergency personnel responding to the scene. Electrical and communications failures spread throughout Lower Manhattan as the collapsing World Trade Center towers took down surrounding infrastructure along with it.

At 11:02, Mayor Giuliani instructed the over 1 million workers and residents in Lower Manhattan to evacuate the area. New York City DOT and the New York Police Department (NYPD) began the process of closing down city streets. The loss of electricity meant that some traffic signals in Lower Manhattan were not operable, requiring NYPD personnel to direct traffic at key intersections.

Figure 5 shows a view of West Street on the afternoon of September 11 with the entire area covered is a layer of soot and ash. Figure 6 is a map showing the status of transportation facilities on the day of September 11. The map shows that most facilities around Manhattan were closed.

With the closing of the subway and rail service approximately an hour and a half after the attack, transit options were limited. With most New York City businesses closing mid-morning for the day, the remaining 2.6 million New

Figure 5. Looking south down West Street on September 11
Source: AP/World WidePhotos

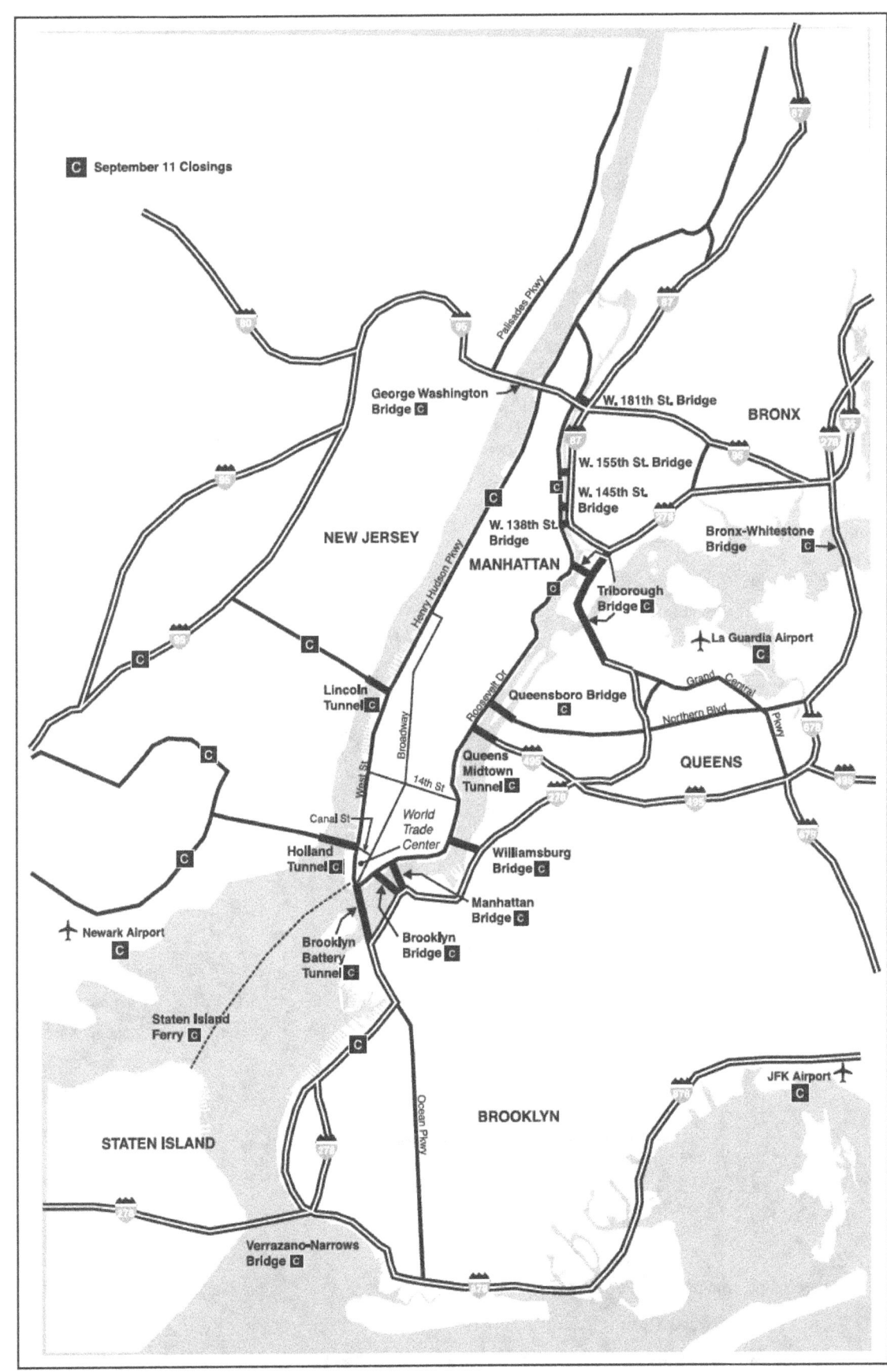

Figure 6. Transportation Conditions on September 11

York City workers outside Lower Manhattan were forced to improvise whatever sequence of trip routes that would get them home. For many, the trip home took several hours longer than normal. Intercity travel ground to a halt as the Federal Aviation Administration (FAA) shut down the commercial air network and Amtrak and bus lines halted service. To facilitate evacuation and emergency response the bridges along the East River were open for pedestrians leaving Manhattan and for emergency vehicles entering Manhattan. The Coast Guard began the process of overseeing a makeshift flotilla of water ferries and private boats to help evacuate people from Lower Manhattan.

September 11, 2001 Chronology- afternoon to night

Time of Day	Elapsed Time	Event/Actions Taken
~ Noon:	[3 hr. 14 min.]	A NYC Transit employee stands in front of Grand Central Terminal with a megaphone to try to dispense advice to travelers.
12:48 p.m.:	[4 hr. 2 min.]	Partial NYC Transit subway service resumes, with many routes truncated or diverted to avoid Lower Manhattan.
1:15 p.m.:	[4 hr. 29 min.]	Long Island RR runs limited service eastbound only from Penn Station.
2:30 p.m.:	[5 hr. 44 min.]	Subway system begins to return to normal except for trains under Lower Manhattan.
3:50 p.m.:	[7 hr. 4 min.]	FEMA activates four urban search and rescue teams in New York.
4:12 p.m.:	[7 hr. 26 min]	PATH service between Newark and Journal Square resumed.
4:40 p.m.:	[7 hr 54 min.]	PATH uptown New York line to New Jersey resumes service.
afternoon:		By evening rush, several public and private water ferry companies are providing additional ferry service to New Jersey, Queens, and Brooklyn, evacuating about 160,000 people from Manhattan.
afternoon:		200,000 phone lines in Lower Manhattan are crippled, telephone and cellular service is overloaded when Verizon central hub at WTC damaged.
5:20 p.m.:	[8 hr. 34 min.]	WTC Building 7, headquarters of NYC Office of Emergency Management (OEM), collapses.
6:00 p.m.:	[9 hr. 14 min.]	Amtrak resumes passenger rail service.
7:02 p.m.:	[10 hr. 16 min.]	Some NY bridges open to outbound traffic.
7:30 p.m.:	[10 hr. 44 min.]	Long Island Rail Road restores full schedule east and westbound.
Nightfall:		750 National Guard troops are in NYC to assist police.
End of day:		65% of subway service is back in operation. Throughout the day, MTA bus service continues running north of Lower Manhattan.
AT&T reports that it has handled the largest one-day volume of calls in its history		

The transportation system that had closed for normal operations was needed to help respond to the needs of the various federal, state, and local emergency response personnel. At this point, it was assumed that those needing medical treatment would number in the thousands, so it was important to keep routes to area hospitals open to emergency vehicles. The Fire Department of the City of New York (FDNY) had 15,000 employees and as many as 11,000 firefighters respond to the WTC attacks. At least 1,000 law enforcement personnel from New York State, surrounding counties, and National Guard police were in New York City by nightfall on September 11th.

By the afternoon, transportation agencies were completing their own internal vulnerability assessments of their facilities and were beginning the process of restoring service to help people leave Manhattan. While Manhattan tunnel and bridge crossings remained closed, transit was slowly returning. By 12:48 partial subway service resumed north of Lower Manhattan. New Jersey Transit had rerouted bus service to pick up people who had taken water ferries from Manhattan. The commuter rail lines began to run limited service out of Manhattan. By night, some river crossings were opened for outbound traffic out of Manhattan.

Figure 7. Ambulances on a Manhattan Street on September 11
Source: AP/World Wide Photo

Evacuating Lower Manhattan

While the evacuation of Lower Manhattan was chaotic, it was an "interesting phenomenon," according to the NYPD. "It happened almost as if it were rehearsed, but no one had ever planned for it. Everyone followed the flow of people leaving the city. The vehicles just followed the people. If you had a car, you just went." The NYPD reported that traffic jams and abandoned vehicles were not a problem in Lower Manhattan. More than likely this was due to the fact that so many people in Lower Manhattan rely on walking or transit, rather than the automobile.

According to the NYPD, the oversight of the evacuation of Lower Manhattan followed a protocol, with the tallest buildings evacuated first. Private companies relied on in-building security personnel to oversee the evacuation, and staff followed pre-practiced evacuation plans.

The in-place evacuation procedure for the City follows a protocol: mass transit shuts down, high threat areas (including bridges and tunnels) are secured, and tunnels and access points are secured for emergency vehicles. Police directed traffic and pedestrians from their regularly posted positions at bridges and tunnels according to this evacuation protocol. Most people initially left the World Trade Center area on foot. Some walked north and, in their search for bridges, discovered piers with ferry service across the Hudson River. Others just seemed to know that "ferries were the quickest way out of Manhattan."

People who were trying to cross into Brooklyn were able to use the series of bridges across the East River. Buses were rerouted to pick up passengers on the Brooklyn side of the bridges and take them to destinations in Staten Island, Queens, Brooklyn and Long Island. Those trying to cross into New Jersey from Manhattan had fewer options because the only river crossings in the area across the Hudson River are tunnels. Therefore people had to rely on the numerous ferries pressed into service that day. One official described the scene on the Hudson River as looking like "the Dunkirk evacuation." Because of the volume of people trying to get across the river, people experienced waits of up to three hours that morning. New Jersey Transit rerouted its service to pick up passengers disembarking on the New Jersey side. Figure 8 shows a Circle Line cruise boat ferrying passengers from Manhattan to New Jersey on September 11.

According to the Port Authority, 160,000 people evacuated New York City on NY Waterway ferries, and 250,000 to 300,000 left by other water transportation, which included Coast Guard vessels and other privately operated dining boats and even tug boats. A retired fire boat evacuated 150 people on September 11, and came back to pump water to the World Trade Center site. This ad hoc flotilla operation was overseen by the U.S. Coast Guard, with the assistance of the Port Authority and NYC DOT.

Meanwhile, traffic was piling up outside Lower Manhattan. Places like the Queensboro Bridge and Holland Tunnel had extensive traffic jams. One New

Figure 8. Ferry Passengers on September 11
Source: AP/World Wide Photo

Yorker tells a story of catching a bus going uptown in Manhattan, thinking it would be faster than walking, "only to sit for 15 minutes at a dead stop in the traffic jam that was moving up 3rd Avenue before the 59th street entrance to the Queensboro bridge." She got out and walked. The Associated Press reported that traffic entering NYC from New Jersey was at a standstill approaching the Holland Tunnel as motorists stood outside their cars and watched the fire. Many morning commuters heading into Manhattan, stranded as the Lincoln Tunnel was shut down to incoming traffic, left their cars to stand on the tunnel on-ramp and watch the smoke pouring from the World Trade Center towers.

The press gave several accounts of the chaos and confusion that followed. According to *Newsday* and *Newsweek*, as the first tower collapses:

> Police close off city streets, creating bottlenecks and bumper-to-bumper traffic for miles. Cars clog streets, mixed with thousands of pedestrians fleeing. Streets are littered with high-heeled shoes, abandoned by women on the run. Two women knock on the window of a closed sporting goods store, pleading for sneakers for the walk home to Queens. Police stop cars to ask drivers leaving Manhattan to take extra passengers, while people taking cabs also take extra

customers. Some of the last few motorists who make it onto the bridges stop to pick up straggling pedestrians. Emergency vehicles occasionally split the mass exodus of people. Commuters devise alternate routes that lengthen their travel in some cases by hours. Thousands jam onto buses and ferries. At the base of the Manhattan Bridge, police prevent people from crossing into Manhattan; pedestrians and motorists are allowed to exit Manhattan by the bridges, but only official vehicles can enter Manhattan.

And as the second tower collapses:

> With police loudspeakers urging drivers on the Whitestone Expressway to keep moving, drivers ignore the order and pull over to watch the second WTC tower collapse. The highway scene is "straight out of a… horror movie. Horns blew, tires screeched, loudspeakers blared, and car radios blared news of the disaster.

The *Washington Post* quotes a fireman at the WTC site when the buildings collapsed:

> It just rained and rained soot, and it was dark. When you see cops running, you know you've got no chance.

On September 11, the Police Department's emergency management plans were compromised when their own high-tech headquarters command center at Police Plaza in Lower Manhattan was forced to evacuate, and many phone, pager, cellular, email, and other communications systems were down or slow. A February 5, 2002, *Newsday* article reported that the NYPD plans to hire an outside consultant to review NYPD response on September 11. Issues of concern include NYPD, FDNY, and Port Authority Police accounts of difficulty controlling and tracking responding personnel, and control problems around the towers' perimeter caused by the intersection of hundreds of people arriving and thousands fleeing.

Taking Action

In general, the NYC Office of Emergency Management (OEM) issued "directives" to transportation agencies and the agencies responded with operating decisions. These operating decisions were communicated among regional agencies by TRANSCOM and on Long Island through INFORM, a New York State DOT traffic management control center, and to the public via regional intelligent transportation systems (ITS) applications as well as television and the Internet. According to the NYPD, "ordinarily there are (coordination) problems within city agencies and between agencies," however, on September 11, there was a tremendous amount of coordination and cooperation between agencies. Table 4, on the following page, summarizes the key decisions made by agencies on September 11.

Table 4. Key Decisions by Agency

Agency	Key Decisions, Coordination, and Communication
FAA	Ordered the closing of the three NYC-area airports. Later, ordered the halt of all aviation traffic across the country.
FEMA	Began the process of implementing response to the "federally declared disaster."
Federal Highway Administration	Implemented "quick release" option for Emergency Relief (ER) funds enabling state and local agencies to send emergency response teams; helped coordinate relationships between state and local agencies.
Coast Guard	Began process of marshalling public and private boats to Manhattan to aid in the water evacuation of Manhattan.
MTA	Coordinated transit closures and re-routed subway trains by maintaining operations staff around-the-clock at the Mayor's OEM who interfaced with Subway Control and Bus Command Centers. Several bus drivers were forced to make "ad hoc" decisions in Manhattan after communications were cut off, buses sustained damage from debris, and hazards blocked roadways.
PANYNJ	Coordinated with FAA to close three major airports: Kennedy, LaGuardia and Newark. Ferry division oversaw ferry operator, NY Waterway; contacted NY Waterway to make sure that vessels were at Battery Park for evacuation; coordinated with Coast Guard and Coast Guard security zone. Bridges and tunnels coordinated with police for closures and EMS access. Closed the water port to freight activity. Shut down PATH service.
NJ Transit	Coordinated trains and closures through OEM at mobile command center.
NY State DOT	Supplied portable VMS, barriers, and backhoes to NYC region with promise of FHWA ER funds; coordinated with INFORM (a NY State DOT facility) for information dissemination; provided temporary offices for NYMTC employees.
NY State Police	Deployed 23 Highway Emergency Local Patrol (HELP) vehicles to locations in Rockland and Westchester Counties; deployed 500 troopers to NYC region (to NYC limits) who cleared highways for EMS vehicles; helped direct EMS vehicles to WTC.
NYC DOT	Worked with police to coordinate closing every road, bridge, and tunnel in Lower Manhattan and show closures on regional VMS; coordinated with NY State DOT out of Queens TMC.
NYC OEM	Coordinated regional response by issuing general "directives" to agency liaisons (police, fire, transportation, etc.) on-site at OEM; coordinated with Governor and FEMA for disaster declaration.
NYPD	Evacuated lower Manhattan by evacuation protocol, tallest buildings first; directed people and traffic from "high threat areas" (bridges and tunnels); secured bridges and tunnels for EMS vehicles.
TRANSCOM	Coordinated closures and reopenings of facilities with various agencies. Issued reports of member agency operating decisions via fax; 800 reports issued in total, terminating on January 21, 2002.
INFORM	Immediately coordinated with police to open up Long Island Expressway for EMS vehicles; displayed traffic information on regional VMS and deployed portable VMS to NYC bridge and tunnel entrances; disseminated traffic reports to local agencies, media, and the public; sent all spare resources to WTC.

Closing a facility

Once the OEM made the decision to close the major transportation facilities leading into Manhattan, it was up to the individual agencies to carry out the action. Given that each tunnel, bridge or other facility is configured differently, facility closure plans varied. In general, the closure involved closing the immediate access to the tunnel portal or bridge span or transit station. For the bridges and tunnels, this was followed by the establishment of upstream diversion points to reroute approaching traffic to highway exits and local streets in advance of the crossing. Remaining traffic in the queue was turned around using toll plaza roadways or any available roadway area and diverting the traffic away from Manhattan. The closure required the cooperation and coordination of agency operations and maintenance staff as well as state and local police. The agencies also immediately contacted Transcom about the status of its facility. Transcom then relayed this information to other agencies and the public.

As an example, the Port Authority decided to close the George Washington Bridge, located in northern Manhattan, minutes after the initial attack. The Port Authority had a pre-existing set of procedures for closing the bridge for incidents, but rarely did it ever close the entire bridge to traffic. Within two minutes of the decision to close down, the bridge's variable message signs (VMS) were flashing messages alerting motorists of the closing. The VMS extends approximately 12 miles on the New Jersey side and as far as the Cross-Bronx Expressway on the New York side of the Hudson River. The signs are located before major decision points so that motorists are able to change their travel routes in the case of a closing. At the same time, Port Authority personnel began the process of closing off the bridge access points and New York and New Jersey state police began the process of closing off interchange connections leading to the bridge. While closing access to the public, the bridge remained open to emergency response vehicles and provided a major link in bringing in equipment for the emergency response effort.

Figure 9, on the following page, gives an overview of the facilities and the closings that occurred on September 11. This map appeared in the September 12 *Washington Post*.

Figure 10, on page 21, indicates the changes made to the subway network in response to the attacks.

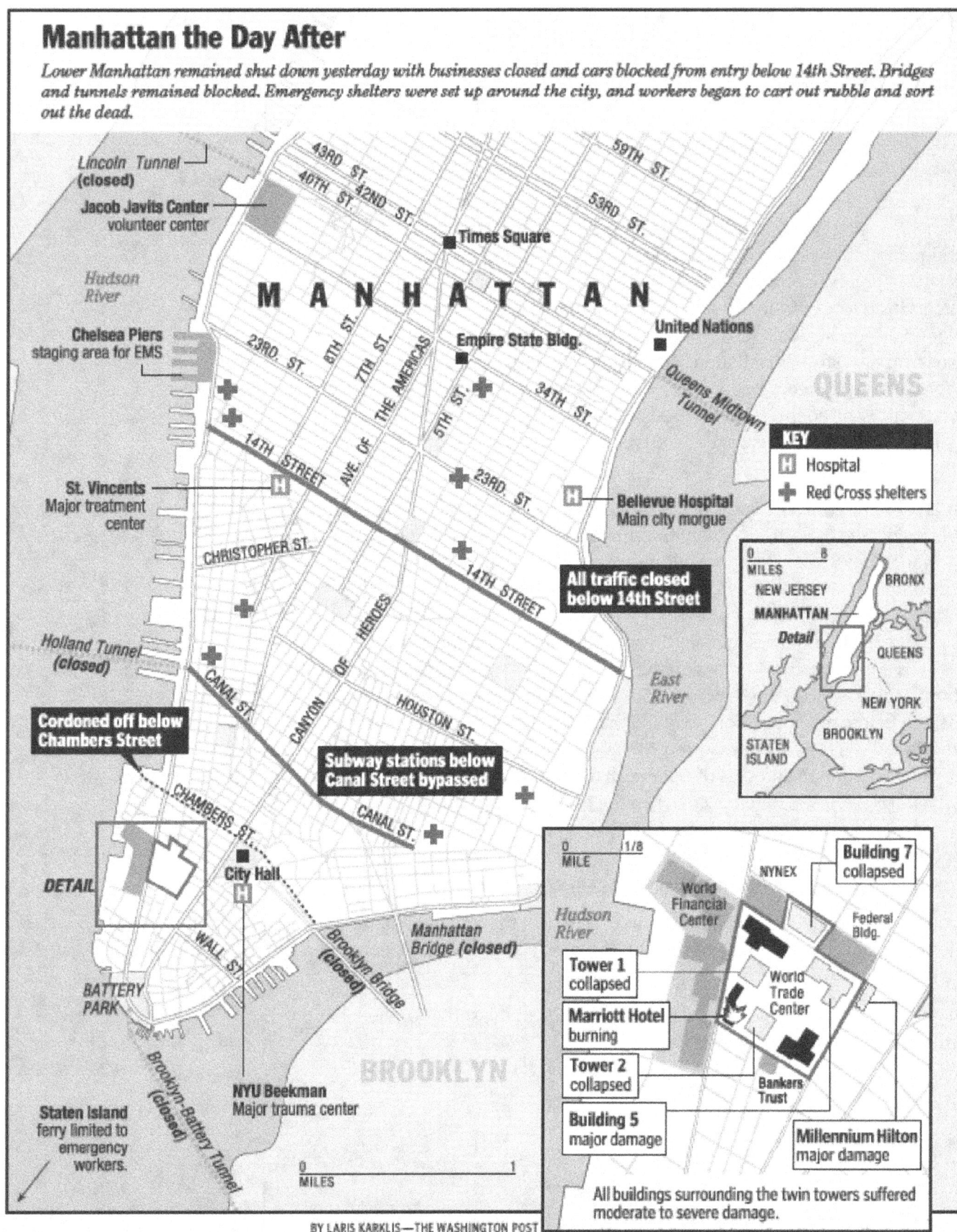

Figure 9. Day After Newspaper Map
Source: The Washington Post

Figure 10. New York City Transit Map of September 24

2.3 Post-Event: After September 11, 2001

Chronology of Events

The following is a brief summary of the events that occurred after the September 11 attacks.

Time of Day	Event/Actions Taken
September 12, 2001 (Day 2)	
8:00 a.m.:	As a result of President Bush's NYC disaster declaration, FEMA's 1-800 help line officially opens.
day:	3,000 National Guard troops are deployed in or near NYC to patrol bridges, tunnels, train stations, and Ground Zero. Mission: protect transportation links.
Day:	MTA Long Island RR and Metro-North RR resume normal weekday service.
Day:	PATH ran free service between Newark and 33rd Street and between Hoboken and 33rd St.
Day:	NJ Transit runs regular commuter rail service, but ridership is only 20% of normal as workers stay home from work.
Day:	George Washington (upper level) and Queensboro bridges open to automobile traffic only.
4:40 p.m.:	The FAA allows airports to reopen on a limited basis for diverted flights.
5:00 p.m.:	Most bridges north of 14th St. reopen.
September 13, 2001 (Day 3)	
3:00 a.m.:	Port Authority reopens the Lincoln Tunnel and the George Washington, Bayonne, and Goethals Bridges and the Outerbridge Crossing
5:00 a.m.:	Port Authority Bus Terminal reopen.
8:00 a.m.	Port Authority reopens water port to freight traffic.
Day:	PATH began to run the 3 services it operates currently- Newark to 33rd St., Hoboken to 33rd St. and Hoboken to Journal Square. (service was no longer free as of this day)
Day:	George Washington Bridge upper level opens. Staten Island bridges open.
Day:	Greyhound announces it is fully operational at all 3,700 locations in the U.S. and Canada.
Day:	Tunnel damage affecting the 1 and 9 subway lines found under the WTC (debris, flooding). Some station entrances on N and R lines are found to be damaged.
Day:	NJ Transit resumes bus service to Port Authority Bus Terminal in Midtown Manhattan, except for two bus routes that serve Lower Manhattan.
Day:	Amtrak increases capacity 30% to accommodate stranded airport passengers.
Day:	Traffic downtown sparse; taxis outnumber cars.
6:00 p.m.:	Working with NYC DOT and OEM, NYC Taxi & Limousine Commission arranges for TLC-licensed vehicles to give free rides to hospitals, blood banks, destinations in restricted areas.
Day:	Two days of bridge, tunnel, and road blockages into Manhattan lead to widespread disruption of commercial deliveries, including FedEx and US Postal Service.

Time of Day	Event/Actions Taken

September 14, 2001 (Day 4)

6:00 a.m.:	Manhattan and Williamsburg Bridges reopen.
11:25 a.m.:	CNN reports all three NY area airports — Kennedy, LaGuardia and Newark — have reopened.
Day:	NY Taxi and Limousine Commission (TLC) establishes 24-hour hotline to address the taxicab and for-hire vehicle (FHV) industries' need for real-time information on access limitations.

September 15, 2001 (Day 5)

Day:	New York City Mayor's Office of Emergency Management moves to Pier 92

September 16, 2001 (Day 6)

Day:	Amtrak and Greyhound report handling twice the normal number of riders systemwide since September 11. Rental cars also report a surge in business.

September 17, 2001 (Day 7)

6:00 a.m.:	Staten Island Ferry service resumes. NYC DOT begins running free ferries: Brooklyn to Manhattan.

September 20, 2001 (Day 10)

Day:	Two Manhattan-bound lanes of the Brooklyn Bridge reopen to private vehicles. Brooklyn-bound lanes remain closed.

September 22, 2001 (Day 12)

	In anticipation of Monday September 24 as the worst day of traffic since 9/11 as commuters fully return to work, NYC DOT urges: use mass transit, "think bikes, think ferries, think subway."

September 26, 2001 (Day 16)

	USDOT requests shippers and transporters of hazardous materials to consider altering routes to avoid populated areas whenever practicable.

September 27, 2001 (Day 17)

6:00 a.m.:	Ban on single-occupancy automobile vehicles (SOV) entering Manhattan weekdays between 6 a.m. and 11 a.m. south of 63rd Street on all East River bridges controlled by the City of New York goes into effect.

September 28, 2001 (Day 18)

3:00 p.m.:	Holland Tunnel reopens to westbound auto and bus traffic. It remained restricted to emergency vehicles in the eastbound direction.
Day:	SOV restriction introduced at the Lincoln Tunnel from 6:00 a.m. to noon weekdays.
Day:	Mayor Giuliani says bridge/tunnel checkpoints set up by police and FBI will remain indefinitely.

September 30, 2001 (Day 20)

Day:	OnStar communications adds real-time traffic reports in a dozen cities, including NYC.

October 4, 2001 (Day 24)

Day:	Port Authority officials say they are hurrying to build a new ferry terminal near Battery Park to cut NJ commute time from 20 minutes to 10.

Time of Day	Event/Actions Taken

October 10, 2001 (Day 30)

8:00 p.m.: City reopens most streets south of Canal St. to regular traffic on weekdays from 8 p.m. to 5 a.m. and all day on weekends.

October 11, 2001 (Day 31)

Day: Port Authority reports that average one-way truck traffic over the George Washington Bridge and Lincoln Tunnel has increased by 1,700 per day.

October 15, 2001 (Day 35)

5:00 a.m.: Holland Tunnel reopened to revenue traffic eastbound, restricted to HOV+2 autos.

October 17, 2001 (Day 37)

Day: Ban on single-occupancy vehicles entering Manhattan is shortened by 1 hour, to end at 10 a.m. on weekdays instead of 11 a.m.

October 28, 2001 (Day 48)

5:00 a.m.: Service restored on the N and R subway lines, bypassing Cortlandt Station indefinitely.

November 4, 2001 (Day 55)

NJ Transit sees 44% increase in ridership in and out of Manhattan after September 11.

Dislocation and relocation of offices from Lower Manhattan and the loss of PATH is causing huge shift in commuting patterns to Midtown.

November 12, 2001 (Day 63)

9:17 a.m.: American Airlines Flight 587 explodes in mid-air, crashing in Queens after takeoff from Kennedy airport.

9:45 a.m.: Port Authority closes: all bridges and tunnels between Manhattan and NJ to private and commercial traffic, its bus terminal in Midtown Manhattan, and PATH rapid transit to NJ.

11:00 a.m.: Outbound traffic from Manhattan is allowed to resume.

12:10 p.m.: Most bridges and tunnels reopen.

December 21, 2001 (Day 102)

NYC DOT reports that public and private ferry ridership has more than doubled since the WTC attacks, from 30,000 to 65,000 daily. Almost a dozen new water ferry routes have been started, with more than 50 boats now in service. In just 6 weeks, Port Authority of NY and NJ has built a new Battery Park dock capable of holding 6 ferry boats.

Reopening a facility

By the early afternoon transportation agencies were beginning the process of reopening their facilities to help people leave Manhattan. During the closure agencies performed vulnerability assessments of their facilities to ensure that there was no damage done and it was safe to reopen to the general public. The decision on when to reopen was coordinated with the OEM and NYPD and information on when each facility would reopen was communicated to other agencies and the public through Transcom.

Because of heightened security concerns, additional safety precautions were taken once the facilities were reopened. City and state police personnel as well as National Guard troops were stationed at key check points to screen vehicles and passengers. In addition, restrictions were imposed on some facilities to ensure that emergency vehicles had priority access and that vehicles that might pose a threat were diverted to certain locations. As an example, trucks were restricted to the upper level of the George Washington Bridge and were not allowed on the Holland Tunnel and Brooklyn Bridge.

While open to general traffic, the George Washington Bridge also served as a major link in providing access for emergency response vehicles. OEM set up a satellite office at the bridge that maintained contact with Ground Zero. Staging areas for supplies and equipment were set up in New Jersey. When these were needed, the information would be relayed from Ground Zero to the OEM office at the bridge and then police would escort the vehicles from the bridge through Manhattan streets to the needed locations.

Transportation Conditions After September 11

In the three months after September 11, the transportation network was slowly returning to normal as mobility was increased and security checkpoints were reduced. Certain segments of the transit infrastructure within the World Trade Center area are still out of service and vehicle restrictions were still in place for Midtown and Lower Manhattan. The airports and water freight port are back in full operation. Figure 12. Transportation Conditions, late Fall 2001, provides a post-event synopsis of the transportation network.

On Saturday, September 15, the Mayor's OEM finally moved its base of operations to the passenger ship terminal Pier 92 on the west side of Midtown Manhattan, where all agencies comprising the emergency response team had an adequate facility from which to direct rebuilding the New York City infrastructure. While not as technologically-sophisticated as its former Emergency Operations Center (EOC) in the World Trade Center, OEM's temporary EOC at Pier 92 contained space and equipment for up to 110 city, state, federal, and private agencies. Among the agencies and organizations that had consoles at the EOC were New York City Departments of Fire, Police, Transportation, Buildings, Health, Citywide Administrative Services, Parks and Recreation, and Environmental Protection, as well as the Economic

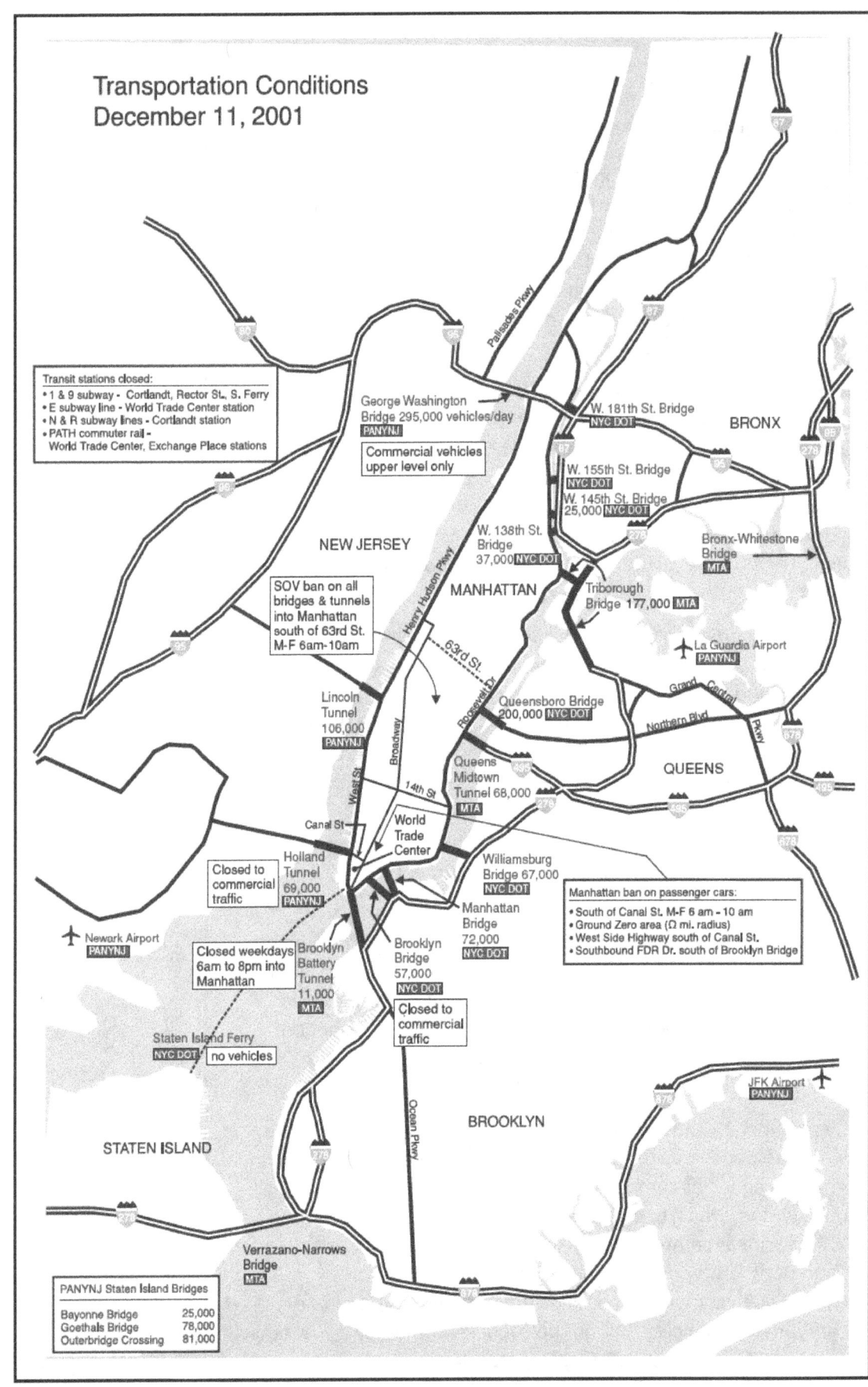

Figure 11. Transportation Conditions, late Fall 2001

Development Corporation (EDC), the New York State Emergency Management Office (SEMO) and the Federal Emergency Management Agency (FEMA). Additional support was provided by representatives from ConEdison, Verizon, and Nextel Communications. The Emergency Operations Center was deactivated on November 23, 2001.

Manhattan Streets

All vehicular traffic was restricted south of Canal Street except for emergency vehicles and authorized buses. Passenger cars were not allowed south of Canal Street between 6 AM - 10 AM, Monday through Friday, nor in the frozen zone by Ground Zero at any time. No pedestrian or vehicular traffic was permitted within about a one-half mile of Ground Zero. The West Side Highway from Canal St. to the Battery Park Underpass was closed to all but High Occupancy Vehicles (HOV) and buses. FDR Drive was closed from the Brooklyn Bridge to the Battery Park Underpass.

Single Occupancy Vehicle (SOV) Restrictions on Automobiles

In the weeks following September 11, traffic congestion leading into and around Manhattan grew worse as vital arteries remained closed, security was enhanced or restrictions remained in place. September 24 through 26 were described by a NYC DOT official as the worst traffic days in the city's history because of the backups due to security checks and facility closings and restrictions. An official was quoted in the September 25 *New York Daily News* saying, "this is the worst traffic day since Henry Ford created the automobile."

NYC DOT officials had estimated that 64% of vehicles crossings into Manhattan were single occupancy automobiles. In response, the Mayor decided to implement a ban on single occupancy automobiles (SOV) crossing bridges and tunnels into Manhattan south of 63rd Street on weekdays between 6 a.m. and 11 a.m. NYC had an HOV plan from the 1980s that was originally designed to help alleviate the effects of transit strikes and was able to be implemented because of the "state of emergency" in Lower Manhattan. As the arterials around the city began to reopen, the SOV plan took effect starting on September 27 with the goal of spreading out the traffic entering the city. Since vehicle counts showed a 23% decrease in traffic south of 63rd Street, the NYC DOT shortened the ban by 1 hour, to end at 10 a.m., starting October 17. Figure 11 shows the traffic impacts of the SOV ban reported by the NYC DOT. They included:

Effect of SOV Ban on Manhattan Bridge and Tunnel Traffic

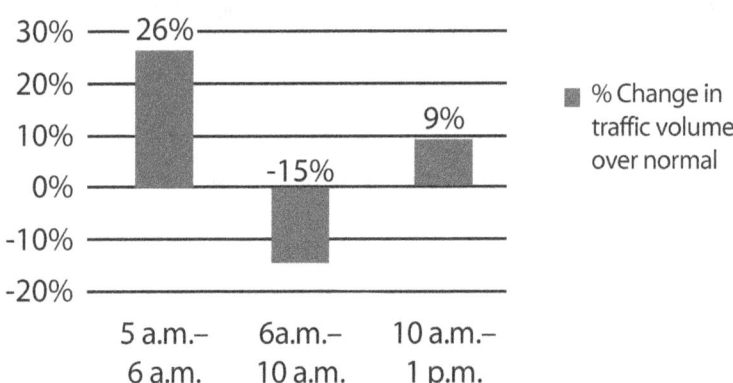

Figure 12. Effect of SOV Ban on Traffic

- 5 AM – 6 AM: no SOV restrictions. Result: a 26% increase in traffic from 5 AM – 6 AM hour

- 6 AM – 10 AM: SOV restrictions in place. Result: a 15% decrease in traffic from normal peak commute

- 10 AM – 2 PM: no SOV restrictions in place. Result: a 9% increase from normal mid-day traffic

The 15% decrease from the normal peak commute (6 AM – 10 AM) shows that the SOV ban did deter some commuters from driving to the city alone or traveling during the peak. The increases in traffic volumes from 10 AM – 1 PM suggest that employers were sensitive to the new commuting restrictions of employees and allowed them to adjust their work schedules accordingly. According to the *New York Times*, city officials estimated that the SOV ban contributed to an overall 30% drop in traffic on bridges on September 30. That figure was down to 23% by October 17, and to 15% by January 3, 2002. ABC TV in New York reported in December that the SOV restrictions were having three effects: an earlier citywide rush hour, additional volumes on bridges above 63rd Street (e.g., George Washington and Triborough bridges) with corresponding longer delays on feeder roads, but an overall reduction in volume of traffic on the highways.

Other Bridge and Tunnel Crossing Restrictions

As of mid-December, commercial vehicles were allowed only on the upper level of the George Washington Bridge. The Holland Tunnel and the Brooklyn Bridge were still closed to commercial traffic. The Brooklyn Battery Tunnel was closed to all Manhattan-bound traffic on weekdays between 6 a.m. and 8 p.m., except for emergency vehicles and express buses.

Vehicle checkpoints were still in effect at Manhattan-bound entrances to the Queens-Midtown Tunnel, all East River Bridges (Brooklyn, Manhattan, Williamsburg, and Queensboro Bridges), and the Lincoln Tunnel.

Transit Operations

PATH's WTC and Exchange Place commuter rail stations remained closed. Because of their proximity to the World Trade Center damage, the following New York City Transit subway stations were closed or lines rerouted:

- 1 & 9 - Cortlandt, Rector Street, and South Ferry stations closed
- E - The World Trade Center subway station closed
- N & R - Cortlandt Street station closed

Thousands of west-of-Hudson commuters who previously used PATH to travel from Penn Station Newark to Lower Manhattan diverted to New Jersey Transit's already crowded trains traveling through Newark to New York Penn Station. For the morning peak period, New Jersey Transit reported ridership growth into New York Penn Station from 33,700 before September 11 to 48,500 in early October. These figures reflected an extraordinary crowding on inbound trains and station platforms. By early December, morning peak ridership had fallen to 43,900 riders.

Ferries

According to the Port Authority, there has been a 91% overall growth in the use of ferry service after September 11, the highest since the 1940s. Originally, the Port Authority contracted with NY Waterway to operate ferry service from New Jersey to the WTC complex to relieve congestion on PATH trains. However, because of its proximity to the WTC, the Battery Park City Ferry Terminal on the Hudson River was closed for 6 weeks to the general public following the attacks. All ferry services were rerouted to Pier 11 on the East River at the base of Wall Street.

To respond to the increased demand for ferry services, the Port Authority concentrated on building more facilities in Lower Manhattan. Specifically, a retrofitted railroad barge was turned into a new ferry landing at Pier A on the Hudson River, near the southernmost tip of Manhattan. The new 6-slip $3.7 million facility at Pier A significantly reduced queuing at Pier 11. With the reopening of the Battery Park terminal and the addition of Pier A, the Lower Manhattan ferries operated by NY Waterway now carry 26,000 daily riders (5,000 through Battery Park and 21,000 through Pier A) where they used to transport only 12,000 (through Battery Park only). In addition, new ferry terminals have been constructed at Pavonia/Newport opposite Lower Manhattan and in South Amboy and Keyport in Southern New Jersey. Figure 13, on the following page, shows the locations of service in the area as of mid-December, 2001.

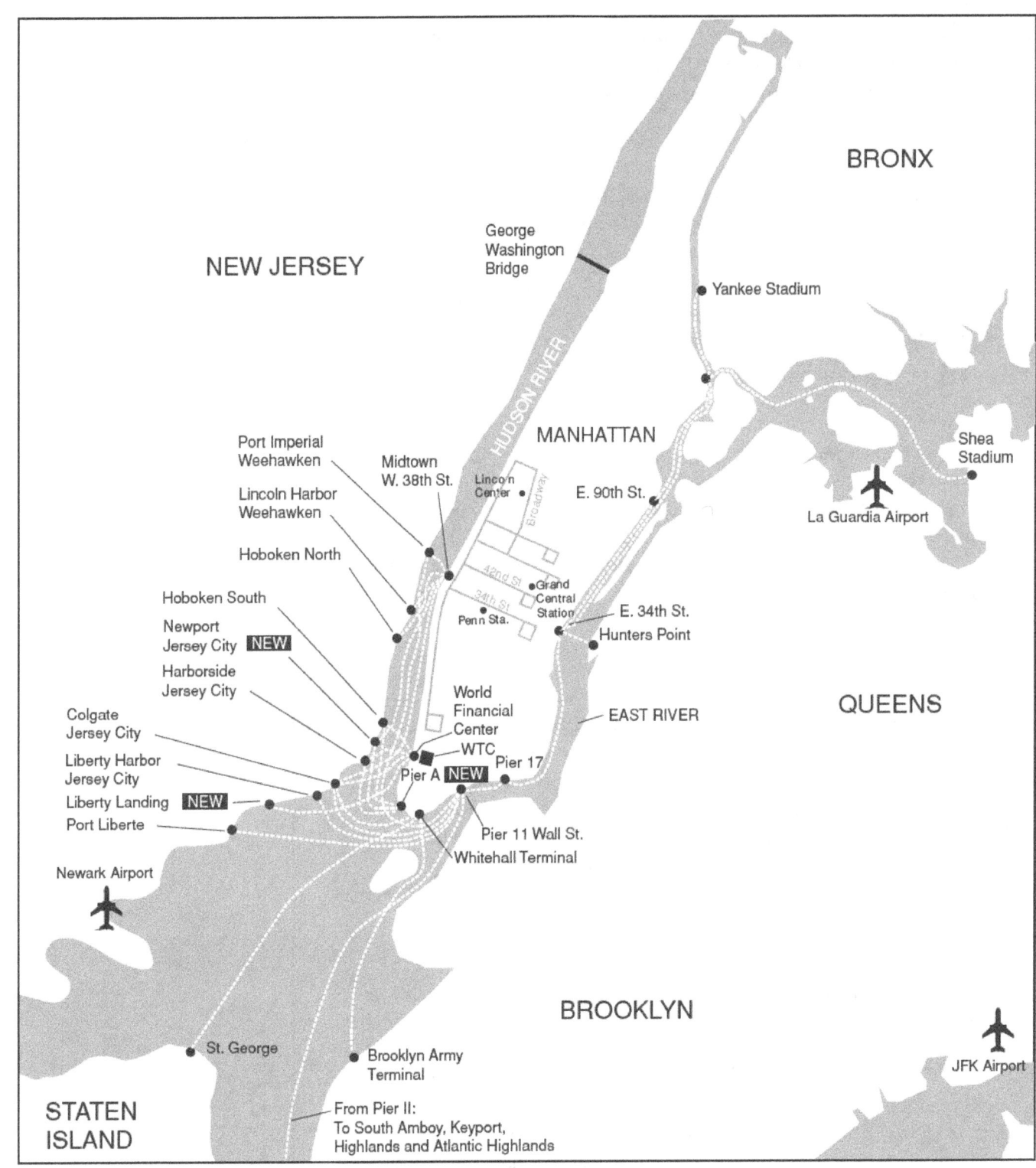

Figure 13. Ferry Service, late Fall 2001

3.0 Findings

Since September 11, the Staten Island Ferry, which previously had carried both passengers and vehicles between Staten Island and Battery Park in Lower Manhattan, no longer permits vehicles, preventing about 1,000 vehicles per day from using the ferry to cross into Manhattan. The main reason for this restriction is to reduce the amount of vehicular traffic in Lower Manhattan.

This section contains the set of findings generated from an analysis of all the information collected in our research and interviews. This report attempts to answer questions about how transportation agencies responded to the attack on September 11 and what lessons were learned. This includes an assessment of the following questions:

- Were the key players prepared?
- What happened?
- Who took action?
- What aspects of the emergency response worked well and why, and what aspects did not work well and why?
- What role did technology play in these aspects with respect to emergency response and recovery?
- What was learned, what could be done differently, and what can be incorporated into the planning process?

Based on this review, four observations were identified:

- **Key Players were somewhat prepared.** Key players were partially prepared because of actions taken in response to the terrorist attack of the World Trade Center in 1993 and other subsequent major and minor events such as the Year 2000 (Y2K) concern, blackouts, special major events, and weather-related events. Actions taken since 1993 included forming a security Task Force in 1993, upgrading emergency procedures, and investing in additional emergency response and communications infrastructure. Although the key players were prepared for standard emergency operations, agencies were not totally prepared for a disaster of the magnitude of the attack. A major shortfall included the lack of true redundancy in key communications and utility systems.

- **Key players made some ad-hoc decisions.** Some of the new infrastructure was destroyed in the attack as emergency control centers and communications hubs located near the WTC were damaged or destroyed. These setbacks forced agencies to make ad-hoc emergency management decisions. Ad-hoc decisionmaking is likely to occur in any type of disaster, albeit at a different scale and frequency. The failure of communications systems experienced on September 11 hindered the ability to quickly make and relay decisions to key personnel.

- **Mayor's OEM coordinated decisionmaking.** In the minutes after the attack, individuals and independent agencies began to take actions on their own. These actions are discussed in the Advance Preparations section. Within a short amount of time, the New York City Office of Emergency Management (OEM) began to take overall control for making and disseminating regional transportation-related decisions. The FBI and FEMA were involved on the Federal level. The OEM was hindered in the first few hours because its Control Center was destroyed and the agency was forced to move four times within the first day.

- **Safety took priority over mobility.** The main focus of transportation operators on September 11 was safety at the expense of mobility. The reinstitution of mobility to the transportation system continues gradually but certain restrictions remain in place.

Some aspects of the response that worked well include:

- The activation of emergency procedures by the transit agencies to ensure the safety of its customers — there was not a single rapid transit-related injury or death on September 11.

- The mobilization of transportation resources to the scene to establish power and communications lines and provide heavy machinery, mobile generators, and skilled personnel helped reestablish vital communications and utility links.

- The ability of field staff to quickly make good decisions on their own in the absence of headquarters personnel.

- The coordinated dissemination of information provided by TRANSCOM.

- Certain forms of communications technology such as Blackberry pagers, e-mail, and two-way radios.

- The transportation system's ability to provide alternative transportation options.

- Intelligent transportation systems (ITS) technology both within and outside of the region.

Some aspects that did not work as well include:

- Relying on Emergency Management Centers that were located in a high threat location. Because the centers were located within the World Trade Center complex they were destroyed and unable to be used during the response and therefore critical time was spent setting up temporary centers.

- Lack of true redundancy in the communications, utility, and emergency response systems.

- Lack of real-time information providing transportation options and updates for public dissemination on the morning of the attack.

- Certain communications networks including landlines and cellular telephones that did not function due to overwhelming demand or damage to the infrastructure.

Five lessons learned that could be incorporated into future planning were also identified:

- **Pre-existing relationships among key personnel are the key to emergency management success.** There is a need for pre-existing relationships both internal to an agency and with other public and private agencies. When asked what role FHWA played in the response, several New York City agencies responded that the greatest help given was the provision of Federal funds and support to regional operational activities over the previous decade. Beginning in the mid 1980s, FHWA provided Federal funding to help nurture regional operations activities such as the I-95 Coalition and TRANSCOM. The coordination of day-to-day operations activities on a regional basis paid dividends during the emergency situation.

- **The need for preparation and training for all shifts of workers under various emergency response scenarios.** Field staff is often forced to make critical decisions with little time for consultation with others. It is imperative that the field staff be given proper training to make the right decision under stressful conditions.

- **An Incident Command System can provide a tool for advance preparations.** The emergency plan used by the New York City region is based on the Incident Command System (ICS) which was adopted by FEMA. This system provides a framework for emergency operations and can serve as the model tool for the command, control, and coordination of resources at an emergency. This plan can be adopted and adapted by communities of any size throughout the nation for various emergencies.

- **Technology aids decisionmaking.** Timely decisionmaking is a function of available information and the communication of that information. The application of ITS to transportation operations can aid in emergency response among public and private agencies and internal and external communications.

- **Essential systems require redundancy.** There is a need to rethink the definition of redundancy. It is important to have additional resources available off-site to ensure the continuous operation of facilities. This was especially important with the emergency management centers in this case. Agencies need backup remote facilities that can be activated if an event damages the primary emergency management center or operations control center. Redundancy is necessary within the transportation system as well as with communications, utilities, personnel, and other facilities.

The findings are grouped into the following sections:

- Advance Preparations and Planning
- Institutional Coordination
- Guiding Priority: Safety
- Communications
- The Role of Advanced Technologies
- System Redundancy and Resiliency.

3.1 Advance Preparations and Planning

Advance emergency preparations were the backbone of New York City's emergency response after the terrorist attacks on September 11. Although the City's emergency response team was not fully prepared for a terrorist attack of the magnitude of that which occurred on September 11, practicing emergency response prior to the attacks for other disasters through the region's Incident Command System (ICS) gave both the agencies involved and the public a high level of confidence in the ability of New York City to manage the emergency situation.

FEMA and the Incident Command System (ICS)

On average, there is a federally declared disaster somewhere in the country once every eight days. In the year 2001 there were 46 federally declared disasters requiring FEMA assistance in 29 states plus Guam and Puerto Rico. The disasters resulted from a variety of conditions including:

- Severe storms
- Floods
- Freezes/Ice Storms
- Tropical storms
- Terrorist attacks
- Earthquakes
- Winter storms
- Tornados

Every disaster requires a coordinated response from local, state, regional, and federal government agencies including those involved in transportation, underscoring the importance of a pre-existing disaster plan for emergency management. Agencies must provide mobility and ensure the safety of emergency response personnel and citizens affected by the disaster.

The ICS was used by New York City to handle response to the World Trade Center attacks. ICS is one of the FEMA-adopted emergency response tools that provides a general plan for managing all types of disasters and subsequent emergencies, yet is adaptable to the specific needs of a community or region.

New York City's Office of Emergency Management (OEM)

Emergency response management starts at the local level where disaster situations are identified, then moves to the state level where the Governor is contacted for assistance, and finally the federal level for Presidential approval and crisis management response and coordination through FEMA for consequence management and through the FBI for investigative responsibilities in terrorist emergencies. The involvement of the FBI affects the way in which the situation is handled, making the response much different from that of a natural disaster. In this case, agencies involved must be flexible in their emergency response procedures, as the emergency rapidly becomes a crime scene.

Although NYC was declared a Federal disaster area, the initial decisions for managing the crisis were initiated by the New York City Office OEM. This multi-jurisdictional agency was created in 1993 to operate as the centerpiece of all New York City emergencies. The Mayor's OEM gives commands to the agencies involved in decision-making, and is responsible for contacting the Governor's office and asking the Governor to declare a "State of Emergency." The OEM comprises personnel drawn from several agencies:

- The Mayor's Office, including the Office for People with Disabilities
- The NYC Police and Fire Departments
- The NYC Department of Transportation
- The NYC Department of Information Technology and Communications
- The NYC Departments of Corrections, Environmental Protection, Parks and Recreation, Buildings, Sanitation, Citywide Administrative Services, and Emergency Medical Service
- The American Red Cross

By following the pre-existing ICS system, NYC's OEM was prepared to quickly manage the crisis as it unfolded. By the end of the day on September 11, the head of FEMA reported that President Bush ordered the release of Federal disaster resources and funds for the New York City region, based on New York

Governor George E. Pataki's expedited request for Federal assistance. This aid supported emergency response efforts to the catastrophic terrorist attacks on the World Trade Center. FEMA followed the U.S. Government Interagency Domestic Terrorism Concept of Operations Plan (CONPLAN) established for such terrorist events leaving the FBI to lead the terrorist investigation and the Justice Department to head crisis management.

Transportation Agency Preparations

Outside the OEM, public agencies (in both New York and the other surrounding states) have detailed emergency response plans that are practiced routinely throughout each year. Private companies also have emergency response procedures and evacuation plans for employees. This was especially true for companies located in the World Trade Center, in response to the 1993 bombing incident. These plans coordinate decision making both internally and externally in conjunction with the OEM. To aid in transportation operations decision-making during emergencies, TRANSCOM disseminates (both internally and externally) the decisions of its 16 transportation and public safety agencies so that they can make informed decisions based on the decisions of partner agencies.

Transportation agencies involved in September 11 emergency response were well equipped to handle the operating decisions required as a result of the general commands issued by the OEM. Agencies placed personnel at the OEM to receive commands firsthand and pass commands to their agency's emergency response center. At agency emergency response centers, key players gathered to make decisions and relay them back to the OEM and TRANSCOM. A Port Authority representative commented that many of the most valuable actions taken on September 11 benefited from having the small things in place, such as people trained in evacuation procedures, having emergency lighting in place, and most importantly, practice.

Key decision makers also had success in dealing with the OEM, other transportation agencies, and the public. After the 1993 bombing, task forces were developed in the metropolitan region allowing transportation agencies to build relationships between agencies and across services to fire, police, and other city departments. These relationships helped support the City's OEM in following the ICS on September 11 and, in general, give the agencies and the public a level of confidence in times of crisis.

The Human Factor in Advanced Preparation

Emergency response plans depend upon the human element for implementation. Although practice in an emergency command center environment is a key element in smooth response to a disaster, human creativity and teamwork become critical when the unpredictable happens. Every emergency can be different in its complexity and personnel are often required to make quick decisions that may have dramatic consequences on the safety of people in the area. The quality of the agency's staff, their ability to work together, and their preparedness at all levels of the organization to handle difficult, changing situations is a key to a successful response.

The FHWA stressed the importance of "knowing your people" in all offices so that you can depend on them in time of crisis. An official at New Jersey Transit noted the importance of "practice, practice, and more practice for emergencies." He also stressed the need to train "not just your first string but also your second and third string because disasters don't always happen Monday through Friday 9 to 5." As seen on September 11, a number of key transportation staff members were either lost or injured that day and the responsibility for decisionmaking fell to others. Staff in the field was confronted with making operations decisions in the minutes and hours after the attack, often without input from senior staff. One field staff noted that "there was no one to talk to at headquarters; it was gone."

The success of the mobilization provided by transportation agencies in helping to evacuate the World Trade Center area on September 11 and the reinstitution of transportation mobility in the days following is not only a testament to the dedication of the management and command center operations staff, but a salute to the teamwork and creativity shown at all levels. The following examples highlight the quick response and creative thinking built into the transportation organizations involved, right down to the field level, that helped save lives while providing mobility for the region.

Figure 14. Subway Station on Morning of Sept. 11
Source: AP/World Wide Photo

At 8:47 a.m., an R train subway operator felt the impacts of the crash while in Cortlandt Station and radioed Subway Operations Control Center. NYC Transit immediately implemented emergency procedures. The train personnel ensured that everyone from the platform boarded the train and then expressed the train to City Hall Station. That was the last train to enter or leave Cortlandt Station before it was destroyed during the collapse of the towers.

At 8:52 a.m., six minutes after the first plane crashed in the towers, the PATH service operator began emergency procedures and instructed Manhattan trains to begin the evacuation of the WTC station. By 9:10, three trains had been able to carry everyone from the WTC station to a safe location in New Jersey.

The George Washington Bridge lost all of its land-based outside telephone lines when the central Port Authority communications system at the WTC was destroyed. Bridge personnel realized that the 1-800 telephone lines that were part of their intelligent transportation system were still functioning. If some of these lines were switched to outside lines, the staff would be able to re-establish phone service. When they were in the process of closing the bridge, they spotted a Verizon truck in the traffic. Recognizing an unexpected opportunity, they persuaded the technician to help with their technical needs. A short time later, they had outside telephone lines available for use.

3.2 Institutional Coordination

The pre-existence of well-established interagency relationships among the many transportation and emergency personnel in New York City was one of the most important success factors in managing the post-terrorist situation. The events of 1993 had a significant impact on better preparing New York City agencies for what came on September 11. After the first bombing, task forces were developed in the metropolitan region among transportation agencies and the police and fire departments, all coordinated through the mayor's OEM. Through these task forces, the players had the opportunity to build good professional relationships prior to September 11. These relationships proved to be the major sustaining factor in a crisis situation, and are helpful for any type of crisis. Additionally, since there have been weather incidents and other minor emergencies in the New York City region since the 1993 bombing, professionals have gotten to know each other and practiced emergency procedures.

An event that requires simultaneous closures of multiple facilities in an effective and timely way requires the close coordination of many parties both within and outside each agency. In the case of the Port Authority, it relied on its operations, police and maintenance staff to coordinate the closure of its facilities. In addition, the operation was supported by multiple state and local police agencies, as well as fire departments and emergency services agencies.

Each agency, in addition to its participation in the multi-agency task forces, had

The existence of well-established interagency relationships among the many transportation and emergency personnel in New York City was one of the most important success factors in managing the post-terrorist situation.

also set up internal emergency command centers. For instance, NYC Transit has a general emergency response plan that they use for all emergencies, including for weather (they go into a practiced emergency response mode whenever the temperature drops below 20 degrees F). Staff is assigned to duties at the emergency command center based on a known rotation. This center is totally separate from regular operations and every operating and critical non-operating function is represented, including track, signals, power, and planning. At the emergency command center, decision makers were able to communicate with key players, most importantly the mayor's office and TRANSCOM. The following examples highlight some emergency command decisions made after the September 11 attacks:

- **OEM makes general command decisions.** The OEM made general command decisions, such as closing Lower Manhattan, and passed these decisions to local, state, and federal agencies. OEM includes not only the mayor's office, but also all city emergency service personnel.

- **TRANSCOM communicates operating decisions.** TRANSCOM then communicated the operating decisions of its 16 agencies among them, issuing reports on the decisions of each agency and allowing all the other agencies to adjust accordingly. These updates were as frequent as once an hour during the first week after the attack. As other public and private entities recognized the importance of the information, more and more requested to be put on the transmission list. TRANSCOM reported that, over a short period of time, it went from providing information to about 40 agencies to communicating with over 400 organizations. These additional groups included various media outlets, private transportation firms and associations that could then disseminate the information among its members or to the public.

- **I-95 Corridor Coalition coordinates travel on Interstate Highway 95.** Working with TRANSCOM, the coalition provided information sharing between agencies regarding incidents, events, traffic conditions, and delays and coordinated messages and requests for congestion management and highway advisory radio between various agencies along the I-95 Corridor from Maine to Delaware.

- **FEMA sends personnel, FBI assumes overall command.** The FEMA command center in World Trade Center Building 7 was destroyed during the attacks; however, FEMA liaisons were on-site immediately. The FBI assumed command since the World Trade Center was quickly designated a crime scene.

- **FAA closes airports.** JFK, LaGuardia, Newark followed FAA procedures for the shutdown. The airports have standard procedures for closing due to snow storms, hurricanes, etc. that they implement. Immediately after the second plane crashed into the towers, the general managers of the three airports spoke with each other and decided to shut down the airports immediately. New Jersey Transit provided additional buses to help get passengers out of Newark airport.

Coordinating emergency response with the private sector is another important piece of institutional coordination. TRANSCOM is an important link for public and private transportation operators because it communicates member agency decisions to public and private agencies throughout the region.

Just as public agencies made operating decisions based on general emergency commands, private operators, too, made individual operating decisions based on the events and the decisions of the agencies around them and the general commands issued by the NYC OEM and the FBI. Amtrak, for example, suspended service nationwide for a top-to-bottom security sweep, Greyhound Bus Lines canceled operations and shut down terminals, Bloomingdale's department store remained open to serve as shelter to stranded employees, Marriott evacuated all NYC hotels, and by the evening hours, Circle Line Tours and the New York Waterway provided free ferry service to New Jersey, Queens, and Brooklyn, evacuating 160,000 people from Manhattan.

The Role of the FHWA

The FHWA acted quickly to begin to coordinate the road relief effort as well as the efforts of other agencies involved in emergency response. Normally, FHWA would also start working with its state and local partners to begin the process to remove debris from the roadways, but due to the nature and the extent of the terrorist attacks, the FHWA authorized FEMA to coordinate debris removal while beginning to coordinate the NY State DOT, FTA, EPA, and FEMA for restoration efforts. The presence of the FHWA and their immediate promise of emergency relief (ER) funds (the quick release option made these funds available in one day) gave the NY State DOT the ability to immediately send construction personnel to Lower Manhattan. The FHWA also served as mediator and helped solve problems that arose between the state and local agencies involved with emergency response.

In the weeks and months that followed the terrorist attacks, FHWA action to rebuild the highway system was mostly kept on hold until debris and wreckage were cleared. Even three months later, the event is "still happening," in that the destruction of the highway network continues to grow with every debris-hauling truck or temporary asphalt surface laid. The FHWA estimates that about one-half of the damage to the highway system occurred on September 11, the other one-half will result from short-term mitigation efforts to aid the rescue efforts. Because of the temporary "fixes" used to aid search and rescue efforts (an additional one foot of asphalt, for example, laid on the West Side

Highway), it is difficult to assess the total structural damage of the NYC highway network. However, NYC DOT and NY State DOT damage inspection reports submitted in January 2002 estimate that permanent repair of federal-aid highways will cost around $242 million.

Even though the FHWA had to rely on temporary highway fixes to allow crews to access the World Trade Center in the months following September 11, the role the FHWA played in coordinating agency relationships before September was long-term and sustaining. Transportation agencies involved in the emergency response noted the pre-September 11 importance of the FHWA in helping to nurture the relationships between agencies that were so valuable on September 11. Two agencies that played a crucial role in disseminating information to transportation agencies and the media were TRANSCOM and the I-95 Corridor Coalition.

3.3 Guiding Priority: Safety

Because of the nature of the event on September 11, the top priority in the hours and days after the attack was safety. This meant that security was increased to protect people and facilities from further harm. Mobility for passenger and freight traffic was restricted as safety took priority. On the national level, the FBI took the lead in protecting the site and deciding what should remain open and what should be closed. On the local level, the Mayor's OEM was the central decision making body. The transportation officials responded to the needs of emergency personnel in deciding what facilities to open and close. Their primary goal was to support the needs of the police, fire, and emergency rescue agencies, which included two actions:

- ◆ Allow priority access for emergency vehicles and personnel to and from the site.

- ◆ Give transportation agencies time to inspect their own facilities to ensure the safety of the facility from possible further attack.

Within two hours of the first plane crash and in some cases minutes, most of the major transportation facilities in Manhattan were closed. This included all the major bridges and tunnels into and out of Manhattan, most local streets below Canal Street and all airports in the region. The transit system, with the exception of local MTA buses, was closed.

While closed to the general public, the facilities remained open to provide mobility for the emergency response efforts on September 11 and the months following. The agencies coordinated with the OEM to ensure that personnel and equipment were able to quickly arrive at the scene. The Holland Tunnel became a crucial access point from the west and the Brooklyn Battery Tunnel from the east. In the months following, facility closures allowed for prioritized debris removal, which tremendously assisted in shrinking the frozen zone over time.

These closings presented a logistical nightmare for transportation officials, as they had to deal with aiding hundreds of thousands of people in leaving Manhattan while providing transportation corridors for emergency personnel. The major forms of transportation for people for the several hours after the attack were walking, city buses, and water ferry service. Even though the closing imposed a great inconvenience upon the traveling public, there was broad public support and understanding for the need to place safety over mobility. As time passed and officials ensured that proper safety measures were in place, transportation officials were able to increase mobility. Some restrictions are still in place.

One of the many dramatic statistics from the day is that not a single rail customer sustained an injury on the transit system on September 11. The emphasis on safety over mobility contained within the existing emergency response plans of the regional transportation agencies allowed transportation personnel to quickly respond on their own. Security of the transportation system after the September 11 attacks went hand-in-hand with safety, and continues to be a priority to this day.

3.4 Communications

Communications immediately after the September 11 attacks were a challenge for transportation agencies coordinating emergency response procedures. Transportation agencies had to focus on the following primary communications needs:

- Immediate emergency response and communication with field staff
- Internal agency decisions
- External decision dissemination (to OEM and to TRANSCOM)
- Public information dissemination.

Immediate communication with agency field staff directly involved in the September 11 attacks was difficult because landlines were damaged and cellular communications systems were overloaded. Agencies in Lower Manhattan using landlines and standard cellular service were unable to communicate with field staff. Two-way radios helped field personnel communicate during the evacuation; however, field personnel without radio communications were out of touch.

New technologies provided communication alternatives that proved successful in the emergency response effort for internal agency decisions. Internal e-mail, for example, helped agencies communicate decisions with their staff. The Port Authority effectively used Nextel phones, especially the direct connect feature. Blackberry pagers (interactive pagers with e-mail capability) were, however, the most successful form of communications on

September 11, according to several transportation agencies. Blackberry pagers work differently than traditional landline voice communications.

Traditional landline voice communications require an open circuit between two people for communications to take place in real time. Data technology, including the internet and electronic messaging used in Blackberry pagers, uses packet switching where a message is broken down into discrete packets of data that may move over hundreds of different channels simultaneously, and rejoins them at their destination. This enables data communication to avoid bottlenecks by automatically rerouting information packets to open routes when a closed channel is encountered, and then reassembling the message at its final destination.

Agency communication centers were also successful in supporting both internal agency decision-making and external communication. Both NYC Transit and NJ Transit had "mobile" communication centers (transit buses equipped with satellite and computer technology), which were used as command posts for communications and decision-making. (New York Transit monitored some of its subway stations from its mobile command post using CCTV.) Along with representatives at OEM, the mobile command vehicles and other agency emergency operation centers gave agencies the ability to make operational decisions and communicate them with OEM and TRANSCOM. (The NY State DOT traffic command centers (TMC) located outside of Lower Manhattan also proved to be successful in communicating and disseminating agency decisions both internally and with the public through ITS applications. Both TMC's are discussed more thoroughly in section 3.5).

Agency communications with the public were also an important part of September 11 emergency response. The public need for information is evident in the statistics. At 9 a.m. on September 11, New York Times, ABC News, and CNN websites saw 0% availability due to demand for information; MSNBC was at 22% availability with a 38-second wait to connect; USA Today was 18% available, with a 47-second connect time. Figure 15 on the following page gives an estimate of the magnitude of increase in website usage on September 11. By the end of the day, CNN reported 9 million hits *per hour* on its website when it normally sees 11 million hits *per day*; MSNBC reported a tenfold increase in Internet traffic; Yahoo reported a 40-fold increase in traffic; Cingular Wireless, the second largest US wireless carrier, reported a 1000% increase in calls in NY; AT&T long distance reported twice its normal workday traffic. Even after the September 11 attacks, the MTA reported 10 million hits on its web site in one day, five times the normal volume, underscoring the need for timely public information on agency websites. The website www.MetroCommute.com was also utilized by travelers. MetroCommute picks up CCTV images from the Interregion Video Network (IRVIN) and INFORM cameras (see ITS Traffic Management Centers) and posts them on its website giving travelers access to real-time information on the web. NYC DOT's Traffic Management Center in Long Island City, Queens, has 55 CCTVs trained on

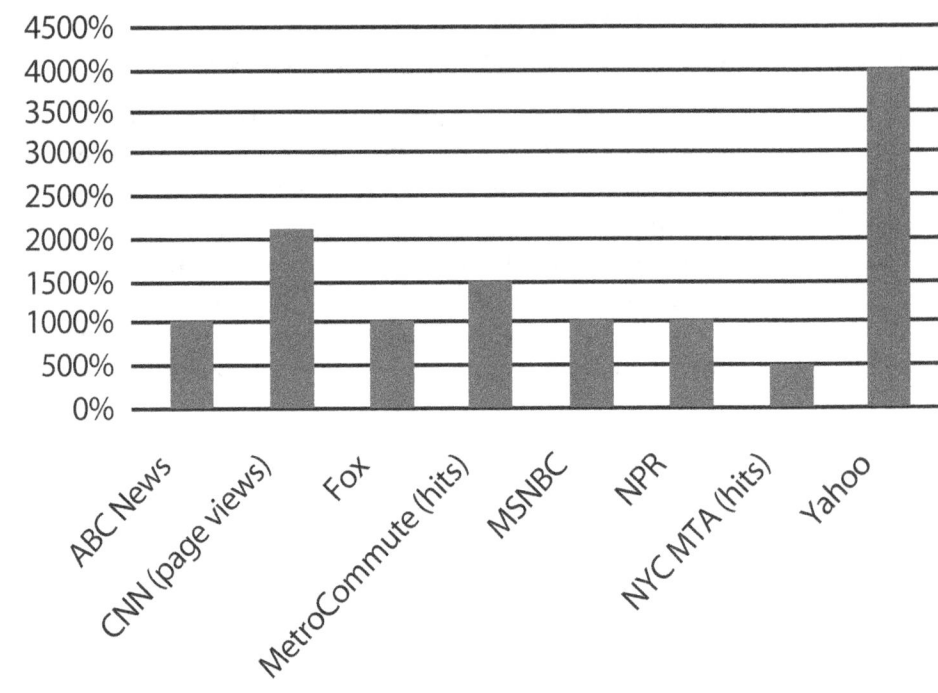

Figure 15. Increase in Web Usage Sept. 11
Note: ABC, Fox, NPR reported 'over 1000%'

major arteries. It also controls 6,000 of the 11,000 traffic signals in NYC via computer. All 2,650 traffic signals in Manhattan are computerized.

Although the Internet was an important means of communication, *USA Today* reported that during the week of September 11, 80% of Americans got their information from TV, 11% from radio, and 3% from the Internet. Overall Internet usage dropped from 58% to 51% on September 11 and 12. Internet sites were slow or inaccessible as demand for information soared. Therefore, agencies utilized radio, TV, and newspapers on September 11 to communicate public information as well. INFORM and TRANSCOM Highway Advisory Radio (HAR) gave up-to-date traveler information and news stations ran INFORM and TRANSCOM reports on the 5:00 news. Local media were also extremely helpful in communicating transportation information, running the story on the SOV ban on page 1 of the *New York Times*, for example. On the other hand, the media could also be critical of actions taken or not taken. The *New York Times* interviewed Michael Powell, chairman of the Federal Communications Commission, who admitted that the audio-only Emergency Alert System was never activated on September 11 because the system was scooped by the TV media. As a result, "public warning" experts called for a system that delivers a wider variety of targeted messages and better coordination between the public and emergency officials.

Agencies also used maps, station clerks, and other staff to relay public information. The MTA reported printing 1.5 million each of "take-ones" (one-page handouts noting changes or updates) and black and white maps in two 12-hour shifts to inform passengers of route changes. Figure 16 is an example of the numerous take-ones produced by New York City Transit to keep customers up to date on the changing conditions of subway and bus service. During the first three days of the disaster, there were over 40 changes to subway service in New York City.

Subway service to lower Manhattan

Mon and Tue Sep 17 and 18

There are no C N R Z or 9 trains.

2 3 run local between 96 and Canal Sts only. Franklin, Chambers Sts and Park Place are closed.

1 runs between 242 and 14 Sts only. Trains run local between 242 and 96 Sts and express between 96 and 14 Sts. Cortlandt, Rector Sts, and South Ferry stations are closed.

E trains stop at all C stations in lower Manhattan, except Chambers St.

2 4 5 6 A E J M service is operating to lower Manhattan, but some stations are closed.

For service *to* nearby stations, use the chart below.

Closed station	Take this train	To this nearby station
City Hall N R	J M	Chambers St
	4 5 6	Brooklyn Bridge-City Hall
Chambers St A C E 1 2 3 9	2 3 4 5 A E J M	Fulton St-Bdwy-Nassau St
Park Place 2 3	2 3 4 5 A E J M	Fulton St-Bdwy-Nassau St
World Trade Center E	2 3 4 5 A E J M	Fulton St-Bdwy-Nassau St
Cortlandt St N R 1 9	2 3 4 5 A E J M	Fulton St-Bdwy-Nassau St
Wall St-Bdwy 4 5	J M	Broad St
	4 5 A E J M	Fulton St-Bdwy-Nassau St
	2 3	Wall St-William St
Rector St N R 1 9	J M	Broad St
	2 3	Wall St-William St
Whitehall St N R	4 5	Bowling Green
	J M	Broad St
South Ferry 1 9	4 5	Bowling Green

Travel information: 718 330-1234, 24 hours

For Monday and Tuesday Sep 17, 18 Post at All Stations

www.mta.nyc.ny.us

Service Notice

New York City Transit

Figure 16: Subway Service Notice- Sept 17

The Port Authority immediately arranged with Verizon to have their toll-free customer information phone number rerouted to Jersey City with basic telephone instruments. Without any capability to have normal telephone menu options or recordings at the outset, the operation was established as a purely manual system, requiring staffing around the clock to handle a tremendous volume of calls. Within 24 hours after the attacks, Port Authority staff began a 24-hour service to answer customer questions and address concerns.

3.5 The Role of Advanced Technologies

On September 11, many of the region's communications systems were out of service or severely burdened from overwhelming demand. Within minutes of the attack, there was an extraordinary demand for accurate, timely information. ITS aided in providing this information by assisting decision-makers in these ways:

- Helped make better informed decisions on when and how to open or restrict facilities.
- Aided better communications with other public and private agencies involved in the response.
- Assisted in communicating with the public about the status of the transportation system.

One of the successes of the ITS was its ability to alert motorists of problems long before they reached the Manhattan area. Both customers and facility operators benefited in having traffic diverted before it reached the bridges or tunnels. After TRANSCOM alerted I-95 Corridor member agencies of problems in the New York City region, these agencies used highway advisory radio (HAR), and VMS on I-95 as far south as Delaware and as far north as New Haven were flashing alerts to avoid the New York City region.

Data from traffic sensors also played an important role. Traffic along key sections of the roadway system including bridges leading to Manhattan was measured, and the information was used to help determine changes in the hours of the lower Manhattan crossings SOV ban.

VMS were also used to communicate real-time information to travelers. Within 2 minutes of the decision to close the George Washington Bridge, the VMS component of the bridge's ITS package was able to alert motorists 10 miles away of the closing of the bridges. Because of the coordinated nature of the ITS package, the information provided by its 1-800 telephone lines was simultaneously updated and the information was electronically transmitted to TRANSCOM for broader dissemination. Figure 17 gives an example of the type of message broadcast to the traveling public on September 11.

Figure 17. VMS on Evening of September 11
Source: Port Authority

In contrast, the Holland and Lincoln Tunnels are not equipped with the same level of ITS technology as the George Washington Bridge and so the tunnel operators require far more hands-on manual monitoring of conditions to provide up-to-date status reports of tunnel operations. For security reasons, since September 11, trucks are restricted to the upper level of the George Washington Bridge and are banned at the Holland Tunnel. The George Washington bridge officials are able to use ITS capabilities to alert truckers of the restrictions long before they reach the bridge. They are achieving a 99% compliance rate because of the success of the VMS. The Holland and Lincoln Tunnels rely on a combination of fixed and portable variable message signs that are not part of a comprehensive automated system as is available at the George Washington Bridge.

During the weeks after the attack, New York City Transit used its web to help keep customers informed. It posted updated maps and service changes. It used its geographic information systems (GIS) mapping capabilities to produce and distribute changes both electronically and by handing out paper "take-one" maps of service changes several times a day.

In response to the attacks, at least one transportation authority is looking at how security components can be integrated with existing ITS and added to the proposed ITS extensions. Prior ITS installation was done mainly for operations but is flexible enough to be adapted for security applications. Television monitors can be modified to provide station emergency evacuation procedures and other security notices. The existing series of traffic operations cameras throughout the region can be used for security monitoring as well as traffic operations. The existing weather monitoring system on the George Washington Bridge could be used to help with hazardous material incidents by providing accurate weather information such as wind direction.

While these useful forms of ITS are provided by the public sector, the private sector plays a significant role in providing other forms of traveler information including in-vehicle communications and navigations that could be used in emergency situations. On September 30, OnStar Communications, for example, added real-time traffic reports to its in-vehicle navigation services in a dozen cities, including New York City.

Figure 18. IRVN Screen Shot
Source: Transcom

Traffic Management Centers

The New York City region has 13 Traffic Management Centers that are linked with each other and capable of sharing data and video feeds through Transcom's Interagency Remote Video Network (IRVN). The IRVN system has approximately 270 video feeds in the New York, New Jersey and Connecticut region. This technology allowed agencies to view incidents on other facilities and make changes to their own operations in response. Figure 18 shows a list of the different TMCs linked into the network and has video shots of four different locations on the New York State Thruway. MetroCommute also utilizes the IRVN pictures and posts them on their website, www.metrocommute.com. Local television stations picks up CCTV pictures and posts images during its traffic reports.

New York City traffic management centers (TMC) located outside of Lower Manhattan proved to be successful in communicating and disseminating agency decisions both internally and with the public. Both the multi-agency TMC in Queens (ITS technology covering New York City streets) and the NY State DOT's TMC in Long Island (INFORM technology covering Long Island highways) served as command centers for state DOT personnel and local liaisons from NYC DOT, NYPD, and NY State Police, as well as sites of public information dissemination via their ITS applications. Communications at both centers were working properly on September 11 allowing for automated dissemination of traveler information.

The Queens TMC, which includes NY State DOT, NYC DOT, and NYPD staff, served as a critical mechanism for traveler information in Lower Manhattan (Region 11). The city's street and highway network was "totally paralyzed" with major crossings and exits closed. According to the NY State DOT, "ITS provided the only mechanism to get people out of the city and continue to warn them of (travel) restrictions." Although the TMC applications were critical, NY State DOT found that there were not enough ITS applications in place in Manhattan. (The TMC is in early deployment stages.) To overcome fixed VMS deficiencies, the TMC deployed portable construction VMS and sent personnel to change messages by hand. After September 11, all new VMS purchased (including temporary construction VMS) will have remote access to eliminate the need for manual operations.

INFORM is a TMC that proved effective in providing real-time traffic information to Long Island travelers on September 11. INFORM technologies cover all major Long Island highways reaching to about 10 miles from Lower Manhattan (near Shea Stadium and the National Tennis Center, Region 10) and include 132 permanent VMS, 28 portable VMS, 2 HAR, and 112 CCTV. On September 11, the INFORM control room was fully staffed and contained TV monitors that showed not only the Long Island highways, but also the New York City skyline and CNN. The TV's pick up images from the IRVN. These images allowed INFORM to weed through the misinformation and report accurate information to transportation agencies and to the public through their transportation reports, which are similar to the regional reports issued by TRANSCOM.

3.6 System Redundancy and Resiliency

The ability to respond to an emergency in a timely and effective way is significantly enhanced through advance preparation, including measures to assure that back-up systems are in place for a variety of critical elements that support rescue, evacuation, and other activities. In the event of an emergency that compromises the quality or timing of the response due to a failure in one of these areas, public safety and welfare are jeopardized and lives may be lost as a result.

Redundancy, the ability to invoke backup for critical systems that fail, either partially or entirely, is highly important to consider in the development of a process or a plan for emergency response. The backup systems invoked for use in an emergency are determined by the nature and scope of the emergency itself. For example, communications systems failure would be less likely in a bio-terrorism event than for, say, the events of September 11. Likewise, the same level of communications failure would not have happened if the targeted buildings in New York City had been different. Nonetheless, because we must prepare for all types of emergency, it is critical that redundancy be built into systems vulnerable to such failures. It is also important to rethink how redundancy is defined. As an example, the Brooklyn Battery Tunnel a redundant system of electricity powering its lights and ventilation system. The Manhattan half of the tunnel was powered from an electrical substation in Manhattan and the other half was powered from Brooklyn. After the attack, the Manhattan half lost its electrical power and that portion of the 1.7 mile tunnel lost its lighting and ventilation systems. When the smoke and ash from the collapsed buildings flowed into the tunnel, people were forced to abandon their vehicles in the tunnel and run to the Brooklyn side.

The topic of redundancy is covered in more depth in each of the sections on Advance Preparations, Institutional Coordination, and Communications. Emergency response planners should consider the following in designing redundancy into their emergency plans:

- The regional transportation network
- Agency personnel
- Communications
- Utilities
- Control centers.

The redundancy of the transportation system in New York helped evacuate Lower Manhattan on September 11 and restore mobility in the days following.

The area is not dependent upon only one form of transportation. The automobile is only one of many transportation options. On September 11, when the tunnels, bridges, roadways, and subways were temporarily closed, local MTA buses continued running above Canal Street, water ferries were pressed into expanded service, and people walked. The MTA was able to restore subway service by early afternoon on September 11 because of the redundancy it has in its subway tunnels.

The need for redundancy in personnel was highlighted when a number of key transportation decision makers were lost or temporarily missing in the attack. Critical decisions were made by personnel in the field who, at times, were cut off from communications with headquarters.

The communications system was severely disrupted on September 11. NYC Transit was able to use its separate system to provide landline telephone service to local, state, and federal emergency agencies when Verizon's network was disabled. On that day, some communications systems worked better than others. Having the option to use various technologies including two-way radio, Internet, pagers, e-mail, voice, and cell phone technology allowed agencies to adapt to the constantly changing landscape.

All of the Port Authorities tunnels and bridges are part of the E-ZPass system, a regional electronic toll collection system along the Northeast Corridor. The Port Authorities primary process center for its facilities was located in the World Trade Center and destroyed. Fortunately, the Authority had a pre-existing, off-site, back-up system and was able to test the system and have it back on line by the time its tunnels and bridges reopened in the early morning of September 13.

Redundant mobile generators allowed for restoration of power to emergency control centers and allowed agencies to begin flood prevention efforts to preserve communications and subway tunnels from extensive water damage.

Redundant control centers helped enormously. Even though the NYC Mayor's OEM Command Center was destroyed when 7 World Trade Center collapsed, nearly every other major agency in NYC had an emergency control center that swung into action immediately. In order to achieve better redundancy and resiliency within the OEM Command Center itself, current New York City Mayor Michael Bloomberg advocates opening five "Help Centers" (one in each borough) that bring together all city, state, and federal services, with desks for every department, commission, and agency, and with a mayoral appointee on site and in charge. These Help Centers would also function as five ready-made Emergency Command Centers for any disaster, no matter where in the City it occurs.

4.0 Conclusion

In response to the events of September 11, officials, including transportation officials, in the New York City area had to make numerous decisions. Their decisions were based on their primary goal: to ensure the safety of rescue workers and the general public. These officials restricted access to New York City and Lower Manhattan, closed bridges and highways, temporarily shut down the transit system, banned motor vehicles on some ferry lines, and instituted security checkpoints. Even though these restrictions imposed a great inconvenience upon the traveling public, there was broad public support and understanding for the need to make safety the first priority.

Advanced emergency preparations were the backbone of New York City's response on September 11. Representatives of several transportation agencies noted that documented and practiced emergency response procedures could have never accommodated for a catastrophic event with such widespread impacts. But it is clear that practicing and preparing for less-significant emergencies did, in fact, help transportation agencies manage and adapt to September 11. Multi-institutional coordination was key. Reliable communication mechanisms were crucial and advanced technologies aided decision makers and travelers in many ways. The redundancy of the New York City highway and transit networks was also a key factor in responding to the emergency.

Although New York City area transportation officials were able to respond to the incredible challenge on September 11, new lessons were learned and additional changes need to be implemented. Given their prior exposure and their implementation of many changes since 1993, New York City officials probably were more adept in responding to terrorist attacks than those in other areas might have been. Officials in other areas should become aware of the events of September 11 and other catastrophic events to ensure that they too are able to successfully manage any future catastrophes.

Practicing and preparing for other emergencies helped transportation agencies respond to September 11.

List of Acronyms

AASHTO	American Association of State Highway and Transportation Officials
APTA	American Public Transportation Association
ATIS	Automated Traveler Information System
CCTV	Closed circuit television
CMS	Changeable message sign
CNN	Cable News Network
CONPLAN	U.S. Government Interagency Domestic Terrorism Concept of Operations Plan
DEST	Domestic Emergency Support Team
DOD	Department of Defense
DOE	Department of Energy
DOJ	Department of Justice
DOT	Department of Transportation
EMS	Emergency Medical Services
EOC	Emergency Operations Center
EPA	Environmental Protection Agency
ER	Emergency Relief
FAA	Federal Aviation Administration
FBI	Federal Bureau of Investigation
FCC	Federal Communications Commission
FDNY	Fire Department City of New York
FEMA	Federal Emergency Management Agency
FHWA	Federal Highway Administration
FHV	For-hire vehicle
FRA	Federal Railroad Administration
FTA	Federal Transit Administration
GIS	Geographic Information Systems
GW	George Washington Bridge

HAR	Highway Advisory Radio
HELP	Highway Emergency Local Patrol
HHS	Department of Health and Human Services
ICS	Incident Command System
IEN	Information Exchange Network
INFORM	Information FOR Motorists
IRVIN	Interregion Video Network
ITS	Intelligent Transportation System
JIC	Joint Information Center
JOC	Joint Operations Center
LFA	Lead Federal Agency
MPO	Metropolitan Planning Organization
MTA	Metropolitan Transportation Authority
NYC	New York City
NYMTC	New York Metropolitan Transportation Council
NYPD	New York Police Department
NYT	New York Times
OEM	Office of Emergency Management
OIC	Operations Information Center
PANYNJ	Port Authority of New York and New Jersey
PATH	Port Authority Trans-Hudson Corporation
PDA	Preliminary Damage Assessment
RRIS	Rapid Response Information System
SEMO	State Emergency Management Office
SIOC	Strategic Information and Operations Center
SOV	Single occupancy vehicle
TLC	Taxi and Limousine Commission
TMC	Traffic management center
TRANSCOM	Transportation Operations Coordinating Committee

TRB	Transportation Research Board
TWC	Time Warner Cable
USCG	United States Coast Guard
VMS	Variable messaging system / variable message sign
WMD	Weapons of mass destruction
WTC	World Trade Center